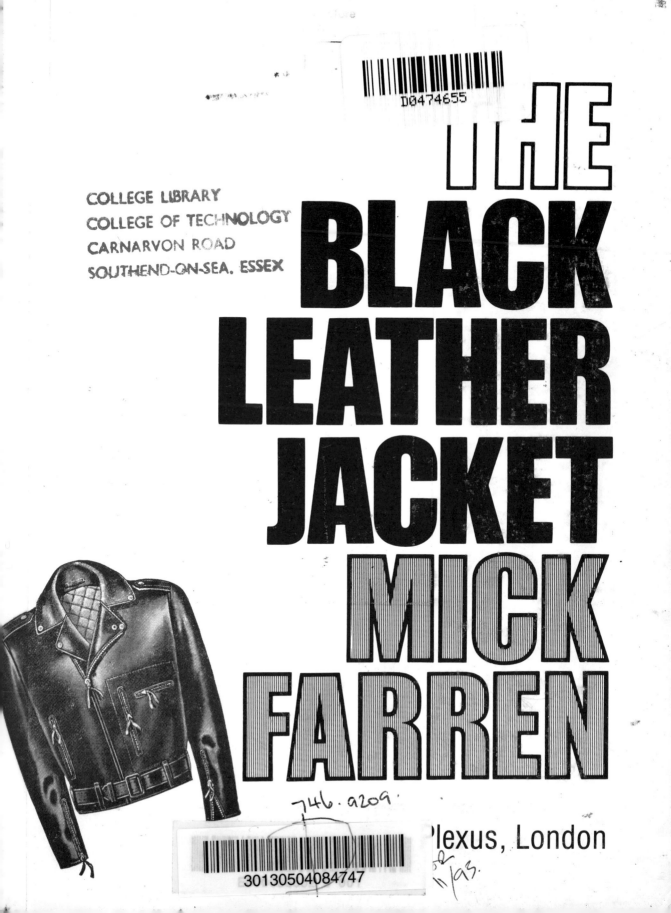

THE BLACK LEATHER JACKET

MICK FARREN

Plexus, London

Farren, Mick
 The black leather jacket
 1. Leather garments—Social aspects 2. Coats
 —Social aspects 3. Black—Social aspects
 I. Title
 391 TT595

 ISBN 0–85965–115–0
 ISBN 0–85965–087–1 Pbk

Cover design: Phil Smee
Book design: Ken Kitchen

Manufactured in Great Britain by Hollen Street Press

Publisher's Acknowledgement
We would like to thank the following photographers, editors,
designers, collectors, picture agencies and fashion houses, for
their help and enthusiasm with the selecting of photographs
for this book.
    Alex Lascelles of The Kobal Collection, *Sounds*, Lewis
Leathers, EMAP National Publications, London Features
International, Camera Press, Syndication International, The
Photo Source, the Imperial War Museum, Nautic Visual
Services, Popperfoto, DC Comics, British Film Institute,
Schirmer Mosel, Rex Features, Schott Brothers, Harry
Hammond, Michael Putland, Wide World Photos, John
Sutcliffe of Atom Age, Thames Television, Lucasfilm U.K.
Limited, *Back Street Heroes*, Geoff Howard, Robert Ellis,
Chuck Pulin, Chris Wroblewski, Helen Campbell, Caryn
Franklin of *i-D* magazine, Expectations, Grace Lau, Paulo
Nozolino, Andy Phillips, John Ingham, Virginia Turbett,
Warner Brothers, Modern Publicity, Graham Hughes, Jeff
Pine, Katherine Hamnett, Montana, Gianni Versace, Jean-
Pierre Gaultier, Transworld, BBC Hulton Picture Library, and
Ann Matthews and Alex Kroll at *Vogue* magazine.
    We would like to extend our special thanks to Lynn Procter
and Ted Polhemus, John Stewart, Peter Maskell at EMAP
National Publications, Steven Myatt at *Back Street Heroes*,
Adrian Owlett, Kim Peterson and Chris Wroblewski. It has
not always been possible to trace the copyright sources, and
the publisher would be glad to hear from any such
unacknowledged copyright holders.

CONTENTS

Monty Clift, Marlon Brando and James Dean boosting the juvenile image.

LEGENDARY
LEATHER

My first encounter with the power of the black leather jacket came when I was maybe fourteen or fifteen. I can still clearly remember the first time I bought one. I'd seen the older guys in school and on the street who wore them; they were the ones who looked cool and, overtaken by adolescent hero worship, I wanted to be just like them. But part of the attraction was also that the leather jacket was frowned upon, proscribed and legislated against. I'd also seen stills of Marlon Brando in

The black leather jacket became the uniform of the bad boys. Below: *the menacing Gene Vincent.* Opposite: *Marlon Brando in* The Wild One.

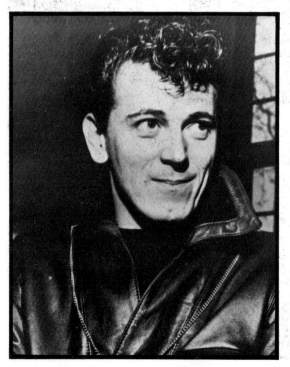

The Wild One, and from the perspective of the time, he was as far as it went. (Marlon was also legislated against. *The Wild One* remained banned in the UK until 1967, presumably to deter young boys like me from emulating the Brando character. It didn't work; it only made me all the more eager.) It was a time when I was seriously fighting the dress code on two fronts. Both my teachers and my folks seemed bent on turning me into a junior gentleman – a potential bank manager or advertising executive if ever you saw one. For my part, I was equally determined to become a greaser hoodlum. It was a time when everything hip and teenage was against the rules, a time of sneaking out of the house with a pair of skintight black jeans hidden under baggy grey flannel pants.

I bought the jacket in a small, backstreet men's clothing store, hard up against a railway bridge in a medium sized seaside town in southern England. It was hardly the concrete jungle but it passed at the time. The store specialized in tacky, juvenile delinquent fashions – polkadot shirts, stardust peggies, dayglo socks and lurid suits that usually fell apart after a couple of weeks. I paid for it out of my own money, cash that I'd squirreled away from what I was paid for crawling out of bed and delivering newspapers at some ungodly hour in the morning. In the prevailing situation, there was no way that my folks were going to spring for a motorcycle jacket and, indeed, there would even be repercussions when I got it home. It was all too obvious that it was my provisional membership card to the Bad Boys, an introduction to the kids they didn't want me hanging out with. I'm sure my normally level-headed mother saw it as the first rash step onto the slippery slope that led all the way down to drugs, degradation and cheap women. So, for that matter, did I. That was why I was so all-fired keen.

It was something of a ceremony. I stood in front of the store's full-length mirror and slipped off whatever jacket I was wearing. (It isn't part of the memory. It was probably some flakey tweed sportcoat of which my mother totally approved.) I struggled into what was going to be my first cool garment. The leather creaked with newness and smelled like the interior of a factory-fresh car but there was more than adequate compensation. It had a red silk lining, just like Dracula's cape. I think I remember making that connection at the time. I also remember the label. The jacket came from D. Lewis Ltd of Great Portland Street, London. It was the Bronx model. As I stared into the mirror, I couldn't believe myself. Admittedly the mirror was tilted up to produce the most flattering effect, but I looked great. My legs seemed longer, my shoulders seemed broader. I flipped the collar up. I looked so damned cool. Mother of God, I was a cross between Elvis and Lord Byron. The old guy who was taking care of me asked me how it felt. I lit a cigarette. I'd been smoking for maybe a year or so, but this was the first time I'd ever lit one while I had an adult's total attention. Jekyll was already becoming Hyde. I told him grandly that it was okay. He really had only the most minimal role in my fantasy.

Of course, to the casual observer, this little scene would have appeared a trifle ridiculous, an awkward kid preening in front of a mirror in a brand new leather jacket. (And there's

nothing so unfortunate as a brand new leather jacket. When I got it back to the neighbourhood there were those who told me to rub it with a brick. This, incidentally, is nonsense. Only time will age a leather jacket.) Much of this leather jacket mystique is a very subjective business. You may be walking around looking like a jerk, but inside you feel like Billy the Kid's bad brother. Even the worst of fools, devoid of all determination and style, can put on the most badly cut, evilly tailored, imitation bike jacket and feel himself capable of taking on the world. It's only when this capability is put to the test that the trouble starts. All too often the world doesn't treat the fool with the seriousness that he believes he deserves, and this is where the seeds of disaster are sown, where the violent, ugly, anti-social punk is created.

I wasn't, however, thinking about any of this. For me, it was an occasion. I was like the young squire in the days of chivalry, receiving his first suit of armour. The cold mornings on my paper round were, I guess, my equivalent of the traditional knight errant wearing out his knees all night in a freezing chapel keeping vigil over his armour and weapons before going out and breaking heads.

· The feeling went with me out onto the street. I'd had the straight sportcoat or whatever wrapped and I was wearing the leather jacket. I immediately felt different. The reflection that glanced back at me from the shop windows and the occasional mirror showed a whole new shape. Boy, at least in his own imagination, had been turned into Man. The whole top half of my body was heavier and more capable while my legs were free, in their tight jeans, to play any games that they could think up. I swaggered, I scowled. The jacket moulded to my moves. The highlights in its finish seemed to accentuate those moves and I fondly believed that I was bad, maybe even menacing. I flattered myself that people were stepping out of my way. Nobody was going to mess with me. Inside my private fantasy, I had moved on from the make-believe world of cowboys and Indians and into the quasi-real world of teen gangs and switchblade justice. Of course, I was extremely young at the time, and I'd just discovered narcissism.

Back in 1973, nostalgia for the 1950s was enjoying one of its many vogues. It's natural that TV should want to cash in one way or another. Over at the ABC television network, they were doing just that, putting together a half-hour comedy called *Happy Days*. It owed a great deal to George Lucas' *American Graffiti*, starting as the story of two middle-class, high school boys living in 1956. There were initial objections to this. It was too much like *Leave it to Beaver* five years on and it lacked a rock 'n' roll dynamic.

The proposed solution was to introduce a third character, a streetsmart greaser in the Dean and Brando mould, to provide a foil to these two boringly straight kids. They had just invented the Fonz. Almost immediately, the producers of *Happy Days* ran into problems. The Standards and Practices department, the network's own, in-house censors, had heard that the character was to ride a motorcycle and wear a black leather jacket. They decreed that a leather jacket should not appear in a sympathetic role on a comedy show that was aimed primarily at children. It was the considered opinion of Standards and Practices that the black leather jacket carried unacceptably strong overtones of violence, criminality and, in some quarters, even homosexuality. They decreed that the Fonz would wear a pale blue nylon windbreaker, and indeed, he had to do this for the first half of the first series until he'd satisfactorily proved himself such a sterling and universally lovable character that he could quietly slip into his leather jacket

Right: *A British rocker.* Inset: *the Ace Cafe, London, a late fifties rocker hangout.*

without objection or comment.

In 1981, in New York City, Mayor Koch and Police Commissioner Maguire were attempting to soften the image of the New York Police Department. In an earlier move, the traditional black and white patrol car had been put into the skyblue and white trim of an ice cream truck. Now the black leather jacket was to be phased out for all but mounted and motorcycle officers. The cops, too, were going into blue, this time dark blue nylon. The rationale was not unlike the one used in the case of the Fonz. Black leather jackets make the NYPD look too much like the Gestapo which, in New York as in many other places, is something that tends to upset people, even those who have nothing on their consciences.

When something like an article of clothing becomes invested with such overbearingly negative connotations that the ABC TV network and the Mayor of New York should feel constrained to move against it, I figure that we can only be dealing with one of two things – perception or magic – or maybe a combination of both.

There can be no doubt that western culture does perceive the black leather jacket as something *bad*. If a band of youth comes shoulder to shoulder down the sidewalk in matching bike jackets, you don't pause to check their haircuts or attitude before you think about crossing the street. The black leather jacket has always been the uniform of the bad. Hitler's Gestapo, the Hell's Angels, the Black Panthers, punk rockers, gay bar cruisers, rock 'n' roll animals and the hardcore mutations of the eighties all adopted it as their own. Marlon Brando used one to boost his juvenile image, as did James Dean, Jim Morrison, Sid Vicious, and the formative Beatles, in addition to every hundred dollar dominatrix who advertises in the back of *Screw* magazine. When Bob Dylan resolved to go electric in 1965, he also decided to slip into a black leather jacket. Dylan, ever – and even overly –

conscious of his public image, certainly knew what he was doing. It was his final yank on the folky's beard and it proved conclusively that he had moved on to the world of rock 'n' roll. In the same way, when Elvis Presley made his 1968 comeback, he got himself done up in black leather to show the rock 'n' roll world that he was back.

There doesn't seem to be any argument that there's something more going on with the black leather jacket than just a simple, utilitarian garment. Divorced from sociology and culture, it doesn't look like much more: waist length, unobtrusive collar, sleeves, a couple of zips, some studs, maybe a buckle or two, ideal protection from the weather for motorcyclists, aviators, anyone with a taste for the rugged outdoors or the wild blue yonder. On the surface, the black leather jacket ought to have a positive and wholesome reputation. In its straightforward form, it has no frills or flounces, no titillating, peek-a-boo slits or anything else custom designed to facilitate crime, violence or psycho-sexual freaky-

Below: *pre-Fonz Henry Winkler, pre-Rambo Sylvester Stallone, in* The Lords of Flatbush. Right: *the real thing*.

12

TWO HUNDRED SE

There was a certain irony that while the juvenile delinquents adopted the leather jacket as their own, so did the local police department.

deaky. By rights, it should be a yeoman garment with no hidden significance. But it isn't.

This inescapable fact leaves us just two basic alternatives. On one hand, we must assume that there's something in the make-up of various kinds of bullies, sociopaths, rock musicians and policemen which gives rise to an overwhelming urge to clothe the top halves of their bodies in shiny black leather. This, however, hardly seems logical. The sweep is simply too great, for the story of the black leather jacket spans at least seven decades and stretches geographically the long way around, from Australian surf punks to the LA Police Department. This has to be more than just a shared taste. If we abandon this argument though, it leads us into somewhat strange territory. We have to conjecture that the garment is somehow able to invest the wearer with a certain power and maybe even bring out the aggression for which people in black leather jackets are significantly famous. Are we faced with the possibility that we may be dealing with actual twentieth century magic?

(You might argue, of course, that the only reason the kid in the leather jacket feels powerful is because people tend to get nervous around young men in leather jackets on account of the garment's previous reputation. This supposes that it all started with one guy in one black jacket beating up one innocent bystander and it all escalated from there. You think so? In this situation I'd rather take magic.)

Not that magic is particularly easy to talk about in this angst-

ridden decade. The 1980s have little truck with mysticism. The bulge babies who once consumed Carlos Castenada like there was no tomorrow (and no yesterday or today, either, all being equal in the cosmic oneness) now cast covert, weary eyes in the direction of retirement plans. Prepackaged cinema nightmares have moved on from *The Exorcist* and the rest of the pop demonology of the seventies to the random psychopath in an ice hockey mask who stalks the girls' dorm with an electric carving knife. The most progressive sector of contemporary music has bailed out from passion and become formalized electronic dance music. *Time* magazine tells us the sexual revolution is all over and the New Celibacy is just around the corner while, in the boutiques, we're faced with either a rerun of yesteryear or visions of the apocalypse.

The use of the word 'magic' has become almost totally secular. Liberace is 'magic', a Hawaiian sunset is 'magic'. The Yankees are 'magic'. Lemon Pledge is 'magic'. The only active 'magic' is conducted by young il-

In Girl On A Motorcycle *Marianne Faithfull became the sixties libertine dream*.

lusionists with long hair and spangled jump-suits who make tigers disappear on casino stages in Las Vegas and Atlantic City.

Perhaps, though, the world is not quite as secular as it first appears. If we penetrate the surface and look beneath the mundane, the extraordinary continues to boil as busily as ever. While we may have abandoned Tolkien, we recklessly embrace Stephen King with all his spontaneous combustion, paranormal children and vampire St Bernard dogs. We have a fair idea of what will happen to us if we build our hotel or housing project on an ancient Indian burial ground. UFOs and the ghost of Elvis Presley still vie with Michael Jackson for the cover of the *National Enquirer* and in California you can buy lessons in walking on hot coals. In the middle east we find Islamic fundamentalists prepared to die for Allah. In small town America we find Christian fundamentalists prepared to nuke for Jesus. The Pope crisscrosses the world, holding Catholic Woodstocks. There's still plenty of magic but we fail to recognize it as such.

Much of this lack of recognition is a result of our general insistence to think of magic in strictly medieval, 'eye of newt' terms. Any magic that's going to function in this twilight of the twentieth century has to work in a culture that's frightened of catching cancer from its microwave ovens and that watches *Invasion of the Crab Monsters* on TV reruns. In this context, it becomes much easier to think of the black leather jacket in the context of, if not an active talisman, at least a solid and potentially powerful totem.

However there is a close connection between medieval and modern magic – and it is embodied in the black leather jacket. The parallel between the leather jacket and the armour of the Middle Ages is neither so far-fetched nor romantically fanciful as it might at first appear. Sure, in my case it was an adolescent fantasy, but there was at least a slight factual basis. For a start, a leather jacket does afford a good measure of physical protection. Any motorcyclist sliding along the abrasive surface of the highway having just dropped his bike will attest to this, as will the experienced bar-room brawler, who is well aware that leather is a great deal better protection against knives, brass knuckles, broken bottles, chains and straight-edge razors than seersucker. Armour has always been something that demanded to be taken seriously. Back in the thirteenth century nobody talked flippantly about so-and-so going about 'in metal clothes.' A man in armour really was an individual with whom you didn't mess. At the sight of a man in armour, the patched and threadbare peasant was very well advised to make himself scarce, to hide in the bushes until the human tank had gone by.

It doesn't really matter whether the character in the armour is a crusader in chainmail or a Hell's Angel in a bike jacket. A set of basic principles apply to both. The armour confers both a purpose and an identity. The man in armour is flaunting his power. He might not be out looking for trouble but at least he was well prepared for the eventuality. This has to be part of the obvious appeal to adolescents. The majority of fourteen-year-olds are still searching for a solid identity and a sense of purpose in a world that seems oblivious to their existence. Anything that bestows a sense of power to someone who feels generally powerless has to be attractive. The majority of adolescents – and also a good many adults – would also like to feel that they were individuals with whom people didn't mess. When the world appears hostile and dangerous, it's nice to know that the peasants will run and hide in the bushes when you come swaggering by. There's never a greater need for psychological armour than during the years on either side of puberty.

Both leather and plate armour easily transcend a simple display of identity. A bowling shirt is a display of identity but it hardly evokes any particular fear or inspires awe. The armoured knight and the biker in the leather jacket were and are something a little different. Both put such an emphasis on communicating the idea of power and potential aggression that their garments quickly become a very personal fetish for the wearer. The knight adorns and decorates it to make himself seem even more dashing and dangerous. Medieval armour was decked out with any manner of religious symbols, ladies' favours, good luck charms and fanciful decoration. Henry VIII, in a spare moment between executing his worn-out wives, commissioned a full suit of plate armour to protect his ample bulk that was entirely covered in tiny pornographic engravings.

The decoration of armour and the accompanying shield were part of the complicated system of heraldry. The heraldic quartering of the knight's shield and the cloth surcoat that was frequently worn over the armour clearly stated the fighting man's allegiances, his ancestry and even the legitimacy or otherwise of his birth. In rather ironic parallel, the motorcycle gangs of the modern world also have a kind of surcoat in the familiar sawn-off denim jacket that's worn over the basic black leather. It too carries all manner of formalized information regarding its wearer. It proclaims to the world the name of the club with which he rides and his position in that club's hierarchy, while the degree of unpleasantness of the club logo – death's heads, demons and eagles have always been big with bike clubs – provides a gauge of the collective badness to which they aspire.

While some bike jacket decorations are exactly that, pure decoration, others can indicate, to those familiar with biker paraphernalia, the wearer's preferences in drugs and sexual variation. Back in the sixties, the Hell's Angels – who would seem to be style setters for all but a few of the more flamboyantly exotic black clubs who go in for cowhorns on Viking-style crash helmets – were strong on enamelling USAF pilots' wings in different colours to show they were, among other things, into marijuana, amphetamines and oral sex.

To the vast majority of the general public, the most disturbing part of motorcycle display – and the punk rock display in the late seventies – is the adoption of Nazi regalia. The usual rationalization for this, in both cases, is a statement to the effect that they didn't actually embrace the philosophy or want to set up deathcamps but only use Nazi symbols as something to administer the ultimate shock to the surface dwelling citizens. The Iron Crosses, the swastikas and the Wehrmacht helmets, however, bring us right back into the realm of twentieth century magic. The swastika goes to the very roots of Indo-European symbolism. All the way, almost to prehistory, it has been associated with the sun, fertility and good luck. This was a swastika, though, in which the right angle arms of its crooked cross pointed in an anti-clockwise direction. When, in the 1920s, Joseph Goebbels commissioned the Nazis' basic house style, the cross was reversed. Its arms now pointed clockwise. Whether this was a deliberate act or merely an ill-omened oversight has been debated ever since the birth of the Third Reich. Whichever answer applies, the result was the same. The flipover also reversed the mystic connotations of this historically potent sign. Instead of sun, fertility and good luck, it now represented the diametric opposite. According to the fundamentals of folklore and magic, it stood for darkness, death and an absolute evil. All of which were horribly apt, considering the glazed, lockstep brutality that followed the Nazi banners. Sad to say, the Nazis play an uncomfortably major role in any history of the black leather jacket.

G E R M A N
I N F L U E N C E

Although I don't know for sure, it would seem safe to assume that the Germans were the ones who actually invented the garment that would eventually evolve into the standard black leather jacket. Certainly the Germans have been into leather clothes since way back when. For centuries, Bavarian males have cavorted in Lederhosen, much to the astonishment of outsiders.

Of course, all kinds of leather clothes have been with us since the first caveperson scraped the fur off his or her loincloth. If Hollywood is to be believed, western gunfighters wore close approximations of the motorcycle jacket and the executioner to Elizabeth I wouldn't have looked out of place with Judas Priest. I fear much of this is a cultural imposition deliberately inflicted on

historical fact with an eye on pleasing the teenage audience. If we're going to content ourselves with looking for the roots of the black leather jacket in the twentieth century, then we have to look no further than the German aviators of World War I – the Red Baron and his boys. It's likely that, somewhere along the line, a chic young ace decided that it'd be a spiffing idea to have his tailor run up a cutdown version of the full skirted leather coat that at the time was standard apparel for both flyers and motorcycle dispatch riders. It's also likely that this prototype was designed more for cutting an off-duty dashing figure in war-torn bistros than for actual combat, since the full length usually fleece-lined coat was eminently more suitable for use in the chilly, exposed cockpits of the aircraft of the time.

These daring young men with their flying machines were something of an anomaly during World War I. A thousand feet above the endless filth and grinding horror of the trenches, they floated and fought with a style and panache, even a neo-chivalry that was completely at odds with the obscene slaughter on the ground. If romantic memory is to be believed, they lived in a stylishly unreal world of champagne at night and death in the afternoon. Von Richthofen himself affected a pet lion cub. Herman Goering, in between shooting down the British and French, was laying image-conscious foundations for his eventual excesses as Hitler's deputy – which included, in addition to crimes against hu-

In World War I, black leather was the province of the flying age. In World War II, it became the status symbol of psychopaths. Previous page, left to right: a British World War I pilot; Von Richthofen (centre) with pilots of his pursuit flight. Opposite, left to right: a squadron leader, Adolf Hitler, Field Marshall Edwin Rommel and Dr Goebbels.

The Red Baron. John Philip Law in Von Richthofen and Brown. Inset: *the genuine Manfred Von Richthofen.*

manity, a taste for small boys, pink silk uniforms and morphine.

The German influence is pretty continuous throughout the entire history of the black leather jacket. As well as an obsession with dark, Aryan, quasi-mysticism and an unholy passion for symbols and regalia, they firmly cemented the relationship between menace and black leather. Again we find ourselves in a fantasy of knights in armour. At the core of Nazi mythology there was the pretence that Hitler's armies were somehow a reincarnation of Teutonic crusaders riding through the world of the sub-human hordes. Once more, black leather provided a modern substitute for chainmail and plate armour. The Gestapo, even though they were supposed to be a secret police force, tended to make themselves obvious in slouch hats and ankle length black cowhide. The SS Panzer divisions boosted their world-conquering ambitions with black forage caps, jump boots and natty leather jackets not unlike the ones that would be worn by rockers two decades later. Variations were also adopted by Luftwaffe fighter pilots and even U-boat crews. At the top of the heap, none of the German High Command, including Hitler himself, felt equipped without an extensive leather wardrobe.

Even after the defeat of the Third Reich in 1945, the German leather fetish hardly diminished at all. From *The Third Man* down, pop sagas of the occupation era – love and death among the ruins of Berlin or Hamburg – costumed their villains, (gangsters, black marketeers or war criminals on the run) in Nazi cast-offs. *Femme fatales,* selling themselves for a carton of Luckies, a bottle of Scotch or a pair of nylons were overt in boots and shiney black. Even though Nazism had been crushed the style pervasively lingered. The problem was that they looked so damn cool. The Nazi uniforms, banners and regalia were designed to impart an overwhelming impression of power, and power is always attractive. With little thought to any long term consequences, the mass media continues to exploit that attraction. There are few male movie stars who haven't, at some point in their careers, taken the opportunity to cavort in a Nazi uniform. From Visconti's *The Damned* to Mel Brooks' *The Producers,* the imagery is run out again and again. Even *Star Trek* has an episode in which the Enterprise encounters a planet full of Nazis. (It's called 'Patterns of Force', you trivia obsessives.)

Even without the direct Nazi influence, the Germans have always seemed to possess a knack for forging ahead in black leather fashion. When, in 1956, Horst Buchholz identified himself as the German James Dean in *Die Halbestarken,* he went a stage further than anyone else in a teen gang picture on either side of the Atlantic. He not only had a black leather jacket but also black leather pants, predating Gene Vincent by four years and Jim Morrison by a full decade.

When the Beatles arrived in Hamburg in the late fifties, the Germans were still ahead in the street level leather look. It was only natural that the late Stuart Sutcliffe, who spent a considerable amount of time posing around like James Dean possibly to compensate for his inability to play the bass, should move on to the Horst Buchholz image. Taking the others with him, he basically established the cowboy greaser look that gave the Beatles their first foothold on fame. It was a look that probably played a crucial part in initially attracting Brian Epstein. However, the black leather seems also to have seriously flustered Eppy and he wasted no time in outfitting the band in those stupid Pierre Cardin suits. From the depths of his own neurosis, he believed that leather was a private vice and repellent to all right thinking people.

Adolf Galland, World War II Luftwaffe.

GOLDEN
IDOLS

It wasn't all a matter of the Germans in the aftermath of World War I; the vision of the devil-may-care air ace was firmly lodged in the fantasies of both sides. Where the Germans regimented it and made it a part of Nazism, the British and the Americans – particularly the Americans – made it a part of pop fiction. Any combination of the leather flying jacket, silk scarf and riding boots was accepted as the unofficial habit of a particular kind of freelance adventurer, one who drifted through the world stealing priceless ancient artefacts, endangering species and engaging in espionage and destabilization. In the UK there was Biggles, in America there was Steve Canyon, and it is, of course, the same image that Spielberg resurrected as Indiana Jones.

The pre-hip leather jacket. Below: *Errol Flynn and David Niven in* The Dawn Patrol. Right: *Kirk Douglas lashes out in* Champion.

Despite the overwhelming money he's generated, Indiana Jones was really only one variation of the genre. He was the collegiate end with a battered hat, bullwhip and hiking boots – I'm aware that Indiana Jones has a brown leather jacket but to get through this part of the narrative we'll have to stretch a point – the archaeologist ripping off the native's golden idols in the name of science. There was an airborn breed, typified by the 1930s comic strip *Terry and the Pirates*, that cruised the Pacific, usually in a Catalina flyingboat, tangling with tongs, Japanese agents and Dragon Ladies. Others had leopardskin hat bands, stayed in Africa and had problems with witch-doctors and lost civilizations. Possibly one of the most bizarre was *Blackhawk,* a comic book from 1941 that, despite numerous mutations in style, still continues today. Blackhawk lived on a secret island with his secret squadron, a gang of soldier-of-fortune fighter pilots who flew matched planes and wore nifty, if close to sado-masochistic, black uniforms with hawk decals on their chests and polished jackboots. Blackhawk and his boys were more fascist, both in dress and behaviour, than the fascists they fought.

The genre even extended into the future. In the 1938 movie serial *Buck Rogers,* when Buck and his boy companion Buddy are thawed out from the polar ice after a four hundred year sleep, they emerge trim and together in matching outfits of black leather jackets, jodhpurs and boots.

Invariably, these freelance adventurers were represented in movies, pulps and comic books as the good guys. About the only time they came off as the bad guys was in *Tarzan.* Tarzan, having been raised by apes, had a whole different perspective on wildlife conservation and the exploitation of native peoples.

All, however, was not fantasy. The leather jacket had come home from the war not only as an image, but also as a practical, utilitarian garment. In the thirties it was favoured in America by heavy industry: longshoremen, truck drivers and construction workers. Although functional and durable, it also had a funky flash. In this it marked a definite, if so far unhailed, piece of social progress. Up until then the working man was, pretty much, only allowed to be stylish on his own time. Work-clothes were either shapeless overalls or an ex-Sunday suit, worn and bagged after too many Saturday nights. When function and style were combined in the leather jacket it finally became possible to bring a degree of dash to the daily grind. The other prime example of this happy marriage of function with style is, of course, the leather jacket's kissing cousin, the pair or Levis. Even in the mid-sixties, at the height of mod, no less than Mary Quant admitted that there wasn't a designer walking who could improve on the basic blue-jeans. The lesson that both battle dress and work clothes have taught high fashion all through the twentieth century is that there's a uniquely pure aesthetic in a garment that's designed to fulfil its function.

The leather jacket was something that no longer belonged to any aristocracy or elite. The Red Barons had relinquished it when they went back to their *schlossen* after the war. The leather jacket, outside of the Indiana Jones fantasy and the Nazi reality, was inherited by Joe and Bill on the production line or the loading dock. It proved on this level to be a truly democratic garment. This combination of dash and democracy must have contributed, at least in part, to the way in which the same leather jacket became the unofficial uniform of the International Brigade in the Spanish Civil War. A workers' army beating back the forces of darkness didn't need uniforms, they turned up in the dungarees, work boots and battered hats. Fancy uniforms, braid and decorations were the province of

31

dictators and their storm troopers. Where, during the first war the newsreels had shown the leather jacket on the fashionable backs of posing fliers, now they'd showed it encasing first the optimism and then the bitter but doomed determination of the men who fought Franco.

Life and art finally came full circle when, in 1943, Gary Cooper was cast as Hemingway's American mercenary fighting with Spanish Republicans in the movie version of *For Whom the Bell Tolls*. He's costumed in pretty much the standard, Indiana Jones soldier-of-fortune outfit. Hemingway and director Sam Wood had taken the standard fantasy adventurer, given him a social conscience and placed him a historical context. The rebel had a noble cause and the image, both fictional and real, was indelibly printed on the popular memory.

The imagery of the twenties and thirties was, however, only minor league stuff compared with the way World War II stamped the leather jacket on the mass consciousness, if only for the simplest of all reasons that literally mil-

Left to right: *ambulance drivers in Barcelona, 1937. Cooper in* For Whom The Bell Tolls. *Mason in* Rommel – Desert Fox.

lions were manufactured as part of the war effort. A simple fact like global war doesn't mean that the concept of chic is sublimated to the desire for either conquest or survival. Almost all combatants, with the Nazis in the clear lead, attempted to field the coolest looking armies, with the leather jacket playing a crucial role. It abruptly dumped its romance with the working man as soon as hostilities got underway and became the badge of the elite and the freewheeling. We've already discussed the Nazis with their Gestapo coats and Panzer uniforms, but the fact that the Nazis went in for such cultural overkill doesn't mean that there wasn't plenty of the same kind of posturing going on in the Allied camp. The Battle of Britain fighter pilots and the B17 crews of the thousand bomber raids had their sheepskin-lined numbers. Partisans, guerillas and resistance fighters all used variations of the leather jacket in their somewhat more free-form approach to uniforms. In this they shared the attitudes of the Spanish Civil War fighters of a few years earlier. About the only major belligerents who didn't cleave to leather were the Japanese.

In any war, it is of course the generals who have to be the most chic. In war time they replace movie stars and singers as primary objects of public attention. Men like Patton,

Rommel, MacArthur, Goering and Montgomery developed publicity machines as intensive as that of any modern TV performer. Generals were aware that one of their foremost functions was to stand around looking cool for the news media, either studying maps, encouraging the poor assholes who actually did the fighting, or staring into the distance through fancy binoculars. (Almost a hundred years earlier, after the debacle of the Crimean War, it was discovered that the last thing generals needed was all the risk and trouble of leading their troops into the battle itself.) Since the average general was forced to spend a good deal of time posing, it was only natural that the average general should give not inconsiderable thought to the ideal garment in which to pose. There had been a time when all a general needed to do to prove his quality of leadership was to deck himself out in gold braid and decorations like some martial version of the proverbial downtown Christmas tree. This may have been okay for an era of parades and the odd cavalry charge but, for the funky tech of World War II, it was altogether too dressy.

This was the real, first elevation of the leather jacket to something above merely ordinary clothes. Generals and their advisers spent long hours working on unique and individual approaches to leather casuals for the battle-field. George S. Patton, pin neat as any Nazi, liked his leather jacket almost formal with breeches, gleaming riding boots, a whip and a polished steel helmet; Erwin Rommel presented a capable image, preferring his leathers calf-length; he was probably more concerned with creating the definitive goggle pushed back onto a peaked cap. (Rommel's lack of fuss might have been a reaction to the excess of Hermann Goering's racks of regalia. Goering even went so far as to develop a black leather jacket with contrasting white lapels, a garment that would not resurface until 1977, on London's Carnaby Street, at the height of punk.) Montgomery was basically uninteresting as he attempted to combine his fur-lined bomber jacket with a woolly, uniquely English eccentricity that seemed to work on the front but left him, fashionwise, looking like the kid in school who didn't have a clue. Douglas MacArthur, on the other hand, took such good care of himself and his image that he became, with his elaborately casual jackets, his turned-up collars, his aviator shades and his trademark corncob pipe, the ultimate authority figure for the second half of the twentieth century. His style has been aped by petty dictators, police departments, military establishments, death squads and private security organizations across the western world. Also, by a stretch of slightly warped logic, his establishment machismo was the face side of a coin that would shortly flip and provide an equally standard anti-establishment image.

If the generals were doing it, then everybody else decided that they ought to be doing it too. War had made the generals role models for everyone else. The leather jacket was promoted to the rank of status symbol. It became a prize, something to be stolen, wangled, hustled for and put up as collateral in a poker game. Supply clerks got them, jeep drivers got them. A good looking leather jacket could turn a schlub private into a glamour boy war hero. They were given as gifts, sent home to wives, sweethearts, kid brothers, widows; they were traded, along with chocolates, cigarettes and nylons for plunder and women in the freshly liberated cities.

As a shaky, dazed and damaged world returned to a semblance of civilian life, it found that a by-product of war was a deluge of war surplus clothing. The leather jacket remained the cream of the crop, particularly in the USA,

Fantasy and reality: World War II pilot. Reagan and Flynn in Desperate Journey.

where the conservative brown version became even more the practical mainstay of every kind of working man. Its more dashing and dramatic black cousin was being taken up by two distinct and often opposing groups. On one hand there were the police. All across America, Highway Patrols, State Troopers, County Sheriff's departments and city police, were making the black leather jacket part of their regulation uniforms, with an obvious eye to the post-Patton image. At the opposite extreme, that mysterious intelligence, the grapevine that is the root communication net of all street fashion, and moves so much faster than any organized media, had picked up on the leather jacket, coupled at first with khaki ex-army pants and later with blue-jeans, making it the basic uniform of the emerging breed called hipsters.

(You'll hear a lot of talk about suits – zoot and otherwise – with regard to hipsters. In the main you can ignore it. Apart from among the most affluent of hustlers, the suit is a Saturday night affair. It was the black leather jacket that

dominated Monday through Friday.)

A great many of the images and attitudes that are taken for granted today first crystallized with the hipsters of the late forties and early fifties. Many had returned from the trauma of war to the boom affluence of the new, uneasy peace. This roaring post-war economy freed them from the poverty or total wage slavery that had been the twin norms of the thirties. Expanding mass media informed them as no other generation had been informed before

Left to right: *John Wayne and Paulette God-dard in* Reap The Wild Wind; *Robert Redford in* The Great Waldo Pepper *and* Harrison Ford in Indiana Jones And The Temple of Doom.

and an awful lot of what they saw through this media they didn't particularly like.

There were twin fears that troubled the leaders of the United States immediately after the end of World War II. The first was that the return to a peacetime economy would pre-

37

cipitate a massive depression and extensive unemployment as it had in the twenties and thirties. The second was the more obvious worry regarding how you're going to keep 'em down on the farm now that they've not only seen Paree but also spent a handful of years killing and being killed. The veneer of civilization had to be swiftly reapplied. The answer to the first fear was to keep the economic throttle wide open. Instead of war production there would be a consumer boom and a cold war arms build-up. This would go hand in hand with creating a massive consumer desire and a massive consumer conformity. The authoritarian dream of the late forties and early fifties was a standardization of product. It was a *Leave it to Beaver* vision of a whole nation sharing a standard suit and a standard haircut, a standard home equipped with the standard appliances, standard car, kids and dog. Everyone would watch exactly the same shows from the same new television networks and everyone would share the same ideals, ideas, beliefs and morality.

The spiritual cement in all this would be a belief in a patriarchal God (and a partriarchal President) and an hysterical, almost metaphysical fear of communism, which, in this perfectly standard world, would be easy to detect. The first sign was a deviation from the norm. It was little wonder that the hipsters should revolt in the face of such a soul crusher. What nobody realized at the time was that this revolt in style and attitude would lay the groundwork for the whole counter-culture that extends clear up to now. Without them, it's highly unlikely that, for good or bad, we would have had Elvis Presley, John Belushi, *Rolling Stone,* Sid Vicious, Nastassja Kinski, Clint Eastwood or Divine as we know and knew them.

Every revolt needs a uniform and while it would be a mistake to assume that every hipster had a black leather jacket hanging in the closet, it certainly signified among the hard edge of the movement. The truth of the matter was that hipsters came in all shapes and sizes. We are all familiar with the pork pie hat, bop vision of urban nightlife. This is where the zoot suit and the wrap around shades came in. We're equally familiar with the woolly bohemians with their fog, their amphetamines and their girls who looked like Juliette Greco. Not too many leather jackets here. We tend to disconnect from a lone hipster like Charlie Starkweather, getting his existential jolts by random mass murder up there in the Nebraska badlands, but there's a black leather jacket if ever you saw one. Charlie Starkweather went to the chair telling the Rotary Club to fuck themselves, he was keeping his eyes.

The popular legend, the media hindsight, of the hipster in the leather jacket was a Southern Californian Jack Kerouac winding his way through Big Sur on a Triumph Twin Tiger with paperback Camus in one back pocket of his fatigue pants and a pint of I.W. Harper in the other. The truth was a little more funky and at times a lot more desperate. There was a percentage of men returning from the wars in both Europe and the Pacific who couldn't find it in themselves to go along with the welcome home, pacification programme. It's hard to settle to bagging in a supermarket after you've been the waist gunner in a B17. California was already started on the cult of personal transportation, and the motorcycle was sufficiently non-conformist to be able to make the personal statement that you weren't ready for what mass society had planned.

Here at last was the real black leather jacket and, very soon, events would escalate, as events have a habit of doing when the media are around. Within the space of just a couple of years after the end of World War II, the image of the black leather jacket and motorcycle boots would be irrevocably associated with mayhem and violence, and the image of the black jacketed and dungareed thug would be established as a primary stereotype in the mid-twentieth century's collective consciousness. The 1947 Hollister, California, Fourth of July motorcycle races and hill-climb meet proved to be the first major gathering of a new breed of wild young motorcyclists, many exactly those same ex-GIs who were finding it hard to adjust. Some three to four thousand bike riders showed up for the weekend and discovered that all that stood between them and a re-make of *Sign of the Pagan* was a worried, seven-man police force. Hunter S. Thompson describes the result in his book *Hell's Angels*:

> 'The mob grew more and more unmanageable; by dusk, the whole downtown area was littered with empty, broken beer bottles and the cyclists were staging drag races up and down Main Street. Drunken fist fights developed into full scale brawls. Legend has it that the cyclists literally took over the town, defied the police, manhandled local women, looted the taverns and stomped anyone who got in their way.'

Legend also maintains that it was one particular gang, the Booze Fighters, who initiated the trouble. In this, they seem to qualify as the first organized motorcycle outlaws. It wouldn't be until three years later, in the small California steel town of Fontana, some fifty miles north of Los Angeles, that the Hell's Angels, the media favourites in the field of endeavour, would be founded.

The real life atrocity tale was dressed up and fictionalized by Frank Rooney under the title 'The Cyclists' Raid' for the *Saturday Evening Post*. The short story was, in turn, picked up by producer Stanley Kramer and turned into a script for a projected movie with the title *The Wild One* (1954). *The Wild One* has to be recognized as a landmark in motion pictures and quite possibly a landmark in the popular end of social dynamics. When Marlon Brando, Lee Marvin and their cohorts swaggered into the greedy, tight-assed small town, every teen in the movie house audience was well aware that their very body language was a challenge to smug authority. When Mary Murphy asked Brando what he was rebelling against, the teens knew the answer even before Marlon shrugged 'What've you got?' In the same way, only the most soulless of kids could fail to envy Brando's divine gall when, as he's being beaten by baying vigilante citizens dressed in suits that look as though they were tailored by a lumberjack, manages to sneer, 'My old man hit harder than that.'

The contemporary reception of *The Wild One* seems to have been an early example of the-old-folks-don't-know-but-the-kids-understand. Back in 1954, the majority of the critics seemed unable to get past the idea that it was a movie purely about violence. The British Board of Film Censors even went so far as to ban the movie from that country's screens until 1967. In fact, there is little overt violence in *The Wild One* if you compare it with many of the westerns and war movies of the same era. What seems most likely to have disturbed the critics was that the violence went hand in hand with the threatening sexuality of the badass, leatherclad bikers. Even Brando himself had misgivings about the film's reception: 'We started out to explain the hipster psychology, but somewhere along the way we went off the track. The result was that, instead of finding out why young people tend to bunch into groups that seek expression in violence, all we did was show the violence.'

What even Brando seems to have missed is that *The Wild One* was essentially about a clash of styles, leather jacket against baggy suit if you like; random, cruising sexuality against smug, self-satisfied certainty. What Marlon Brando didn't know at the time was that his costume from the film would prove to be a codification of a youthful rebel uniform. It would remain fixed, with only the slightest mutation, for the next thirty years.

TEENAGE DREAMS

Over on Madison Avenue they were inventing teenagers. Initially it was the Junior Miss fashion industry doing its bit to fuel the postwar boom. The basic idea was define and exploit a unique time between puberty and responsibility. Full employment and an extension of public education had made possible a brief period of twentieth century, mass market self-indulgence before an irrevocable settling down. Whereas, in the past, there'd only been a crude transition from school to workforce, now every human (at least, every white middle class human) had a right to a fleeting age of magic – a *teenage*. The original concept was a pink and white, Barbie & Ken world of cherry cokes, dating, taboos on the erogenous zones and continuous consumption. It was clearly a

hot commercial strategy but Madison Avenue failed to appreciate just how hot it was.

Adolescents always have trouble with their identity. By definition it's a time when you've yet to find out who you are and you try all manner of masks and costumes. The teens of the early fifties had been offered not only an identity but a whole social subgroup in which to play around. J. Walter Thompson's boys couldn't have realized that they were opening the first tiny fissure of what would eventually become the generation gap. Needless to say, the teens just scarfed it up but, proving from the start that youth are ingrate swine, they swiftly ran through what was being offered and started off on their own grubby fantasies.

If an adolescent is anything, he's paranoid. He takes a great comfort from the idea that the world is against him, and likes to assume the importance of rebellion. 'What are you rebelling against?' 'What have you got?' It's almost an expression of need. One of the first images of rebellion available to the kids of 1951 was of those drunken hipsters who trashed Hollister. When the image, the basic black leather jacket and motorcycle boots, was prepackaged in *The Wild One*, it took hold like a brushfire and swept right across the nation. Post-war society was discovering that not all the innovations that could whip through a mass culture are imposed from above. Almost overnight the black jacket emerged with or without a motorcyle, as the accepted uniform of the bad teen and at least eighty per cent of this was accomplished entirely at the grassroots. In most cases, the media lagged far behind, chronicling the phenomenon rather than instigating it. This is why it wasn't until 1955 that Hollywood was able to gratify a huge youth fantasy and come up with an all-purpose compendium of bad teen.

In three films, James Dean personified all that was teen.

James Dean was, of course, the embodiment of the whole deal. Montgomery Clift's vulnerability on one side and Brando's narrow-eyed tough on the other both acted like twin John the Baptists to Dean's confused fifties Cool Jesus. Without a doubt, his best long-term career move was to die young and unsullied. By the simple act of killing himself off in an autowreck, Dean assured himself a much more fixed place in the pop continuum than, say, Marlon Brando. He was an icon, not an actor who went on to play Fletcher Christian, Colonel Kurtz, the Godfather and Superman's dad.

By a strange irony, Dean never wore a black leather jacket in a movie. I have friends who used to wax metaphysical about that and similar stuff, but I tend to take a somewhat more direct approach. It would have been ludicrous if he'd worn one in either *East of Eden* or *Giant*. The only chance he got was in *Rebel Without a Cause* and in that landmark of juvenile angst, he elected for a red nylon windbreaker just like he was Michael Jackson. In the old days, when we were much more hysterical, this was looked at as an omen. The symbolic colour of blood marked the doomed boy-king. Yeah sure. Or maybe it was just so he'd stand out in a cast where every other male – Dennis Hopper, Sal Mineo et al – *was* wearing black leather. How else could the audience spot Dean in the night-time long-shots like the chickie-run sequence? Two times, though, Dean did get to wear a leather jacket on TV, once when he played a 'hep cat killer' in the December, 1954, General Electric Theatre presentation of *I Am a Fool* (in which he co-starred with Ronald Reagan), and again in May 1955 in Schlitz Playhouse's *The Unlighted Road,* when, as yet another crazy mixed-up kid, he died in a hail of authoritarian machine-gun bullets.

Dean also had a black leather jacket in his private life. It seems the least that he could do. That's the story according to John Gilmore who, in 1975, while there was something of a Dean revival in progress, published a slim paperback volume that somewhat belatedly revealed that Dean was, at least in part, gay – 'a lover of men as well as women' as the cover blurb put it. Gilmore even went so far as to include a picture, contemporary to publication, of himself looking decidedly middle-aged, posing beside what purports to be James Dean's very own black leather jacket, displayed hanging on a wire hanger from a nail stuck into the wall beside him.

Rumours of James Dean's homosexuality tended to surface in clumps. In the immediate aftermath of his death the wildest of rumour circulated but none were about his being gay. He was mutilated, disfigured, hiding in a Tibetan monastary, sending spirit messages to a waitress in Grand Rapids, but there was no public whisper that he might have fucked his way to fame through a procession of gay room-mates. The first suggestion came a couple of years later, in a circumspect, fifties way, with William Bast's biography, *James Dean* – by a former room-mate. Two novelizations of Dean's life that came out around 1960, *The Immortal* by Walter Ross (which had a cover by Andy Warhol) and *Farewell My Slightly Tarnished Hero* by Ed Corley, reinforced Bast's suggestion. Kenneth Anger made his famous remark about Dean being a 'human ash tray', and an uneasy heterosexual world perceived an icon slipping away. Young punks, who'd spent most of their puberty squinting into the bathroom mirror trying to reproduce Dean's myopic vulnerability, stopped dead in their tracks. They fled wimpering to more reliable heroes – Clint Eastwood, Burt Reynolds, Joe Strummer.

The gay community was, on the other hand, delighted. A world class teen idol had emerged from the closet, even if posthumously. They were in a position to haul him in and make him their own, a jet-age Saint Sebastian of the Holy Cigarette Burns. The obvious appeal wasn't only a matter of the Dean legend, the hot-house neurosis and the speeding, quasi-sacrificial death. The Dean visual was also an important milestone in gay imagery. During the early, struggling stages of his career, Dean actively cultivated the clean cut, blond, brush-cut athlete look that was such a major theme in the gay pin-ups of the period immediately following World War II. It was a quality that Dean never quite lost even at the height of his brooding prime. In exactly the same way that Dean's screen image stood midpoint between Montgomery Clift's angst and Brando's aggression, as a gay sex symbol he was the link between the Tab Hunter, shower scene jocks (or Marines or sailors or whatever fantasy of boys together) and the new, mysterious black-jacketed kids who were studying to look like Elvis Presley. In fact, it's more than possible that Dean's image planted some of the first seeds that would, over the next two decades, blossom into the leathermen in their straps and caps and handlebar moustaches that are a regulation sub-group on every gay cruising strip in the western world.

(And just to close another of those cosmic circles, Tab Hunter came out of the closet in his late forties and starred in – even sang the title song to – John Walter's *Polyester*.)

The first time I saw Gene Vincent I was but a youth. It must have been one of my very first rock concerts. The tour had started as a double-header, Gene Vincent and Eddie Cochran. By the time it reached the Essoldo, Brighton, Eddie Cochran was something like a month dead and his place on the bill had been taken by an individual called Jerry Keller who was having his fifteen minutes of fame with something called *Here Comes Summer* ('School is out, oh happy day . . .'). Needless to say that he received short shrift from the teds and greasers, the Triumph Bonneville school of criticism, who made up what seemed like

90 per cent of the audience. All memory of him has been completely blotted out. Gene, on the other hand, has remained indelibly engraved. He was the performer who finally removed any doubts I might have had that rock 'n' roll was, when you got down to basics, about anything else but the nasty side of life.

Vincent came on in the first top to toe, black leather suit that I'd ever seen. There was a ring on the outside of his single black glove. His collar was turned up at the back and framed an immaculate DA. An equally perfect bunch of grapes cascaded down his forehead. A gold chain with a heavy gold medallion hung around his neck. He moved with an accentuated limp. The end of a steel leg brace was clearly visible below the cuff of his pants. If, in the teen myths of the time, Elvis Presley was the leader of the pack, Gene Vincent was the psychotic cripple kid who you could bet on being shot dead by the cops well before the end of the last reel. Vincent took all that they could give him and projected it back at the crowd with an intensity that threatened to burn him up. His face was contorted and corpse white. His eyes would swivel heavenwards and he'd appear to quiver as though racked by the energy that was passing through him. With one leg in a brace, Gene couldn't shake like Elvis. From the waist down he was rigid, his damaged leg stuck out behind him, he clung to the microphone for dear life. At moments of extreme stage passion, he would spin through 360 degrees and swing his crippled leg clean over the mike. Like I said before, he radiated nasty. He sang of nasty love with girls in tight skirts and red lipstick, his attitude was one of franticly mindless, juvenile aggression. He had no time for the teenage euphemisms used by the 'acceptable' rock stars. Gene didn't give a damn for acceptable. He had enough problems just singing out his demons.

There is absolutely no doubt that Gene Vincent was the first rock 'n' roller to make black leather a trademark. Forget about Elvis Presley. Presley didn't get himself up in a black leather suit until his NBC-TV special in 1968. Even Vincent didn't start dressing that way until the start of the sixties. In fact, early rock 'n' roll, as with James Dean, proves to be something of a disappointment. Despite what *Happy Days,* Sha Na Na and all those other nostalgic, rose-tinted reconstructions might want us to believe, the rock stars of the fifties didn't walk on stage in leathers. Why should they? The leather jacket only became stage wear in the perverse sixties and raucous seventies. In the fifties, the leather jacket was streetwear. It was for robbery and rumbles, riding a motorcycle, woofing at girls and scowling at the citizens. It was punky daywear. It was the summer of consumerism and even the coolest work-clothes had no place in the spotlight when belting out *Long Tall Sally.* To do so would show about as much class as Frank Sinatra coming onstage in overalls. Then, as now, stagewear was expected to be larger than life. The stage meant gold lamé tuxedoes, lime green mohair suits, drape jackets, cat clothes, high-rise pants and two-tone shoes, certainly not a leather jacket and blue-jeans. Hell, if the performers were dressed like that, how would you tell them from the audience?

It would be nice to think that Gene devised the black leather outfit all by himself but, alas, while Gene might have been the wildcat, he wasn't too much of a thinker. The credit for the image has to go to a British TV producer called Jack Good. Good was the kind of oddball that only England could spawn. He was a particular type of upper middle class enthusiast who, in the normal run of things, would have collected vintage cars, preserved old locomotives or protected rare species of wading birds. Good, however, was in the right place at the right time to become terminally

Below: *Gene Vincent, the rock'n'roll Richard III*. Right: *Bruce Springsteen*.

Below: *Elvis Presley in 1968 for his NBC special. A comeback in black leather.*

gung-ho for rock 'n' roll. Although he had a classical education, he sought a career in television and entered BBC-TV – always a haven for misfits, but also a place where an old school tie can mean more than proletarian considerations like ratings and point shares.

Good set about translating his obsession with rock music to the TV screen. With the almost inhuman luck not only to be working in a field of one but also in a field that was itself a total unknown, he was able to bring the country's first three rock TV show, *6.05 Special, Oh Boy!* and *Boy Meets Girls* to the air. The latter two heavily featured American hard rockers like Vincent, Jerry Lee Lewis, Eddie Cochran and Little Richard, all the ones who had fled to Europe to escape the cultural purges in the USA that were forcibly replacing them with acne clones like Bobby Rydell and Frankie Avalon. It was thus that Good was put in a position to costume Gene Vincent.

Good was becoming tired of the post-Zoot suits and embroidered cowboy shirts that passed for chic among the American stars and longed to experiment with more dramatic, positive images. In Vincent, he was presented with the perfect opportunity. Vincent had arrived in the UK under more of a cloud than most of his contemporaries. With his band the Bluecaps, Sweet Gene had enjoyed a number of American hits but perhaps enjoyed them rather too fully. On tour, they had left a trail of damaged motels, defiled daughters and father and brothers hunting them with shotguns. They seemed to operate in a haze of booze and pills long before it became standard practice in that industry. The penultimate act before his flight to Europe was to play one final TV show in Los Angeles with the Bluecaps and split to Alaska with both the cheque and the band's equipment. It not only broke up the relationship, but also got Vincent blacklisted by the Musicians' Union. In Vincent, Jack Good couldn't have missed that he had someone who wouldn't have too many objec-

tions to a full scale career makeover.

Jack Good had one problem. He was still a closet classicist with a hang-up about hooking his new-found music into what he perceived as the main stream culture. In later life, he'd shoehorn Jerry Lee Lewis into a musical based on Othello called *Catch My Soul*. In Vincent he saw an unholy combination of Hamlet and Richard III.

In actual fact, this was not as insane as it sounds. Laurence Olivier's movie *Richard III* had been released in 1956, almost parallel to the emergence of rock 'n' roll. It had done the rounds of the British school system and Olivier's Richard, with a hunchback, a leer and a foot-dragging limp that wiped out every Igor in cinema history, had been a huge hit with small boys. Working on this comparatively recent memory, Jack Good borrowed Olivier's black outfit, gold chain and medallion, limp and all. White panstick and a tortured expression completed the outfit and Gene was let loose on European TV.

The experiment was an unreserved success. From looking like a southern, small town, pool hall punk, Gene Vincent had been converted into a limping, near supernatural menace. His songs became exercises in frenetic agony. Jack Good didn't manage to insert Gene into the mainstream of pop – Gene Vincent was always too weird for any kind of mainstream – but he did elevate him to major cult status in Britain, France and Germany. Huge, baying crowds of teenage boys treated him as an ideal, badass role model, an ultimate leader of the pack. Although Vincent wasn't actually responsible for introducing the black leather jacket to Europe, he was a major force in promoting it as a symbol of discontented youth. In France, he was challenged by another American expatriate called Vince Taylor who actually brought a lawsuit against Vincent in an attempt to stop him wearing his leathers. He claimed that it was he and not Vincent or Good who had originated the look.

(For those of you who like to hear the end of stories, Gene's success sadly did not last. By 1968 he was a chronic alcoholic and his career had been swamped by rapidly changing styles. He attempted a comeback at the end of the decade under the patronage of Jim Morrison and the Doors but it was more of a novelty outing than a serious return to the spotlight. In 1971 Gene's bad leg was amputated and in the same year, in Hollywood, he died of bleeding ulcers caused by booze. The fate of Vince Taylor is less clear. Some stories have him as a psychedelic casualty, others claim he found Jesus and became a born-again Christian. One way or another, he dropped sufficiently far from sight that he didn't bother or wasn't able to surface when, in 1979, the Clash's recording of his song, *Long Black Cadillac,* kindled a passing interest in his work.)

Did you ever think seriously about *The Avengers?* Of course not. Who would? In fact, what is there to think about? *The Avengers* was nothing more than a classy spy spoof, the thinking person's *Get Smart* that never quite embraced either the sado-sexism of James Bond or the down-at-heel, twilight of empire that was Deighton and Le Carré. It was Carnaby Street and Op Art and girls doing karate and now it's an option on the menu of syndicated re-runs, possibly not as popular as *The Odd Couple* but enough of a curio to continue to recycle in the late-night TV market.

Or could it be that there was a little more to *The Avengers* than merely a psychedelic chuckle? Consider the basic series premise at its absolute face value. When the tongue is removed from the cheek, the whole concept become decidedly warped. Here is the middle-aged secret agent – John Steed – a dapper, more portly Bond in bowler hat and custom clothes. He has more of a Wildean wit but we are led to assume that he's equally deadly. Indeed, Bond and Steed even share a taste for vintage 4-litre, Le Mans Bentleys. Steed's helper is a Mrs Emma Peel. (For the purpose of brevity, I will confine myself to the series of *Avengers* that starred Diana Rigg. Most of the main points that can be applied to her can equally be applied to her predecesser Honor Blackman and her successor Linda Thorson.) Mrs Peel is a perky martial arts expert who likes to dress from head to toe in skintight black leather and whose hobby is counter-espionage – Nancy Drew after graduating through *The Story of O.* It's implied that while in the show's fantasy present Steed and Peel may or may not be lovers (*Mrs* Peel does, in fact, have a long lost husband), sometime in the fantasy past they clearly had a relationship that was quite Byzantine in its erotic unorthodoxy. When all this is read into the essentially comic book set up, the pair of them begin to appear like leftover libertines from the era of De Sade, trying to adapt to a more egalitarian century. They do this by saving the nation from the depredations of mad scientists, sick robots, Russian spies and, in one episode, a defrosted Adolf Hitler, with a dilettante dash that never quite takes itself seriously.

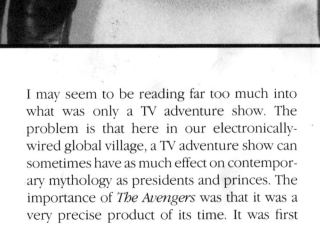

I may seem to be reading far too much into what was only a TV adventure show. The problem is that here in our electronically-wired global village, a TV adventure show can sometimes have as much effect on contemporary mythology as presidents and princes. The importance of *The Avengers* was that it was a very precise product of its time. It was first

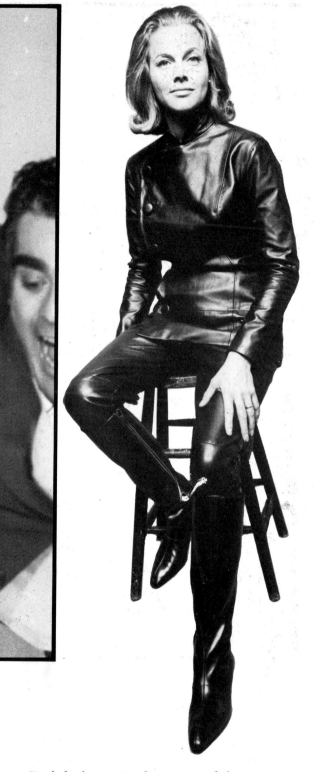

aired in the UK in 1961 but never really mutated into the form we know and admire until around two years later – say 1963. 1963 was the year of the Profumo sex scandals and the fall of the Macmillan government.

As with most scandals, it's hard in retrospect to see what all the fuss was about. It started with a minor political scuffle. It turned out a junior defence minister was entangled in a relationship with an attractive young whore called Christine Keeler. Among Keeler's other clients was a Russian who was suspected of being a KGB agent. Clearly, this was a free game for opposition politicians. When questioned in Parliament about his emotional life, Profumo lied. He knew nothing about hookers. He was caught out in the lie and forced to resign.

Common sense should make it no surprise that the ruling class of any country maintains for itself a covert prostitution party network. What the hell does anyone expect? Unfortunately, the human race seems to have a built-in need to place its leaders on moral pedestals and whenever it's revealed that they are in fact the same grubby brutes as the rest of us, a ripple of shock runs through the community as prurience and prudery clash.

Once the glare of publicity had hit one small nook of this British sex fun circuit, the whole deal started to unravel. Press and TV started digging. Hookers like Keeler, Mandy Rice-Davis and Ronna Ricardo, sensing that a day of reckoning was almost certainly at hand, sold their stories to the lurid London Sunday papers. Stories began to circulate about whips and chains, beatings at a pound a stroke and high heeled boots in high places. Tales were told of an anonymous senior cabinet minister who liked to play servant in a black leather mask and diapers. The word 'kinky' became part of the popular vocabulary. At one extreme there were Polish slumlords and Jamaican pimps selling ganja; at the other was the Royal Family.

Far left: *the original costume of* The Avengers *heroine, later modified as being too risqué.* Centre: *Diana Rigg as Emma Peel.* Above: *Honor Blackman as Cathy Gale.*

The British public seemed to sense that this was more than just a twenty day sex scandal. The moral authority of the traditional ruling class was decayed beyond any repair. It was the end of an era, a realization that the memories of empire had finally to fade. Harold Macmillan, the last Conservative patriarch resigned and the interim premier, Alec Douglas-Home was forced into an election. Harold Wilson came to power in what amounted to a lower middle class revolution.

It wasn't just a matter of Mary Quant and the Beatles, either. All through country and culture, the white man put down his burden and attempted to discover hedonism. If it was good enough for politicians and princes it was good enough for the rest of us. Young men seized the media. Kenneth Tynan said fuck on TV. The once proud Union Jack became a jacket for Pete Townshend.

Large chunks of what had previously been underground bobbed to the surface like grimy ice floes, and nowhere was it more noticeable than in fashion. The high boots, leather skirts and net stockings that had previously been confined to motorcyclists' girlfriends and specialist prostitutes were walking down the High Street. An elderly foot fetishist wrote to one of the skin mags of the time (I believe it was *Penthouse)* complaining how he couldn't get off any more now that what had once been the objects of his dark and secret obsessions were running round in broad daylight. Britain had started down a rather unique path to decadence. The country was going to hell but it was going with the kind of good humoured enthusiasm it had previously reserved for warfare and organized games. Kathy Gale and Emma Peel – quite as much as the musicians and the models, the photographers and the clothes designers – paraded this new, tongue-in-cheek decadence and even marketed it to the rest of the world. Britannia no longer ruled the waves. She

exported rock 'n' roll bands and weird lady spies, each with the costumes of a dominatrix and attitudes of a head girl.

In the sixties, there were a number of groups who couldn't cope with black leather in general and the classic black leather jacket in particular. The symbolism upset them the political connections frightened them and they preferred to pretend that the music that went with it had never existed. A perfect example was the folkies. There was no place for the leather jacket among the CND hootenany set. It didn't look right amid the turtleneck sweaters, the fat men with beards, the ministers, Pete Seeger and skinny girls with straight black hair and Juliette Greco make-up. The folkies were essentially renegade middle class, the black leather always sets off middle class alarm bells; no matter how conscientious and liberated they might be, a greaser couldn't hang around with a bunch of folkie/peaceniks for very long wearing a black leather jacket without one of them calling him a Nazi.

It was essentially a legacy of juvenile class war. The folkies may have taken a left turn at the start of their first year in college, but old instincts don't die that easily. The leather jacket brought back too many memories. Preppies against greasers, fraternity boys against townies, the Italian kids who hung out on the corner and tried to kick your dog. It was okay to bleat on about turn of the century Colorado miners, they were safely enclosed in a Woody Guthrie song. A contemporary apprentice welder, six feet one in a leather jacket, was a whole different matter. He'd put Boots Randolph on the jukebox and, if he got drunk enough, might even punch out your lights and steal your girlfriend.

It took Bob Dylan to put paid to this particular piece of prejudice and drive the wool-wearing folkies out from the foothills of fashion. When, at the 1965 Newport Folk Festival, where the folkies turned ugly when

Dylan walked onto the stage with a big Fender Stratocaster strapped around his neck and a full blown electric band behind him, he was also wearing a black leather jacket. With anyone as intelligent, devious and as conscious of symbolism as Dylan, it seems unlikely that he dressed that way by accident. It was one more poke in the eye, an extra insult to the folkies screaming 'Judas'. He was plainly repudiating the sweaters who'd nurtured him. Bob Dylan had decided to become a rock star and he'd gone back to his leather jacket.

The conflict between the English Mods and Rockers was something very different. It wasn't a matter of class at all. Both groups were working class kids from the same streets, the same schools and the same backgrounds. On average, the Rockers might have been a couple of years older but beyond that there was no demographic separation. The battle was one of pure attitude and pure style. The second wave of youth culture was in physical combat with the first, its own version of the neanderthals and cro-magnons. In one corner you had the Mods – haircuts, mohair and Motown Music; smart and slick. They took to amphetamines and became obsessional on the subject of street fashion. In the other, there were the Rockers – jeans, boots and a leather jacket, a motor-cycle even; stubborn and dirty, they were fixed in the belief that rock died with Buddy Holly. The Mods, with vicious pillhead logic, decided that the Rockers should be exterminated because they were out of date.

At the root of the clash was a basic Mod premise that the Rockers had bought a very dumb portion of the consumer myth. The Mods hadn't seen the young Elvis Presley, they'd only seen *Blue Hawaii* and they were deeply suspicious of the entire deal. Sure it might be great to have all this cheap, disposable stuff but they were well aware that it was only bought with squirrel cage jobs: stockboy,

Bob Dylan and Patti Smith.

mailroom, store clerk. They didn't need Bob Dylan to tell them that a job was being done on them by society's pliers. The Rockers, on the other hand, were massive traditionalists. They'd taken to the black leather jacket, the blue jeans and the motorcycle. They liked them and they saw no reason to give them up just because some new fad had come along. As far as the Rockers were concerned, what was good enough for 1953 was also good enough for 1963. It was this philosophy that caused the Mods to hate the Rockers worse than the rest of regular society. The Rockers were ponderous kids resisting change. The Mod stood for constant evolution; hating Rockers was worthwhile. They were easily identifiable, easily accessible and just as prone to violence. It was possible that this was the world's first consumer war, the street politics of plenty.

Fortunately styles in both politics and drugs changed before genocide could actually take place. By the start of 1967, the Mods were already schisming into two distinct groups. The bright and the trendsetting were experi-

53

Bike jacket decoration became the new heraldry.

'I am the lizard king. I can do anything.'

Lou Reed waiting for his man.

menting with psychedelics, easing paisley and William Morris into their fashion schemes and wondering if there might be a percentage in joining up with the hippies for the duration. The remainder – the ones with the real need for hate – were busy shaving off their hair, buying heavy boots and inventing the sub group that would eventually be known as skinheads. One of the saving graces of the sixties was that things moved so quickly that there was never any time for root fascism to form a united front. Fascism was left to the authorities.

It was, however, a bleak time for the leather jacket. The smart set was now investing in bells, beads, finger cymbals and body paint. The nuclear disarmament symbol was being converted into a tribal totem. Clandestine labs were making the drug STP out of nerve gas. Fey flower children blowing bubbles, playing flutes or just plain looking vacant became a common sight across two thirds of the planet. As if there weren't enough confusion already, fairyland was loose and growing like a cancer. Clearly there was no place for the black leather jacket in fairyland. When most hippies were forced to confront one, they tended to blanch and mutter stuff like 'oh, wow, too aggressive, man'.

Indeed, that might have been the end of the whole thing. The leather jacket would have been relegated to a garment for greasers alone and it would never have given cause for a book like this to be written. Fortunately, life is never that simple. Even the hippies' Tolkien world view was a little more complex than it might have appeared on the surface. They needed clear cut heroes and villains to give a certain dynamic to stoned hallucination, a few barbarians to point up their own cloying goodness. Flirtations were concocted with the most unlikely groups. The Hell's Angels became a regular feature of any large hippie event and the Black Panthers made spectacular entrances on the political edges of the psyche-

delic circus. It was among these objects of danger that the leather jacket retained the potency of its image.

It also wasn't too long before the hippies wanted to start being their own danger symbols as a means of self protection. The world hadn't exactly cottoned on to fairyland. The authorities used any law to hand, particularly the convenience of marijuana prohibition, to harass the hairy youth culture. Rednecks, hard hats, farm boys and other gut level conservatives used tyre irons, bats, boots and dark places to put across a similar message. Lyndon Johnson was either unwilling or unable to halt the Vietnam war and then Richard Nixon was elected President of the USA and there was no use pretending any longer that things were anything but mean. *Easy Rider* romantically enshrined the feeling. The hippies' veneer of peace and love was, after all, not more than eighteen months thick. It cracked as the dopefiends became hostile all over again. Amphetamines and Karl Marx were out on the streets. The word 'revolution' was being loosely bandied about and black leather jackets were being dragged from closets and inspected for mildew by the million. By 1969, the leather jacket only had one rival in street fashion; its close, but less dramatic cousin, the olive drab combat coat. The youth revolt was on and leather had come back into its own. It wasn't just a matter of the boys, either. From Maoist lesbians to rock stars to Brigitte Bardot, everyone was doing the same act.

The big, pop role model for the youth revolt was singer and poet Jim Morrison. This is hardly news. In recent years Morrison has been heavily biographied, so most of the world is well aware that he was a drunk, would fuck just about anything that moved, was into hanging from tall buildings and creative pissing. What tends to be forgotten among all the wealth of scandalous detail and tales of drunken outrage was that the Morrison legend wouldn't have survived as long as it has if he hadn't managed to strike a few very precise chords that resonated and, indeed, continue to resonate in the psyche of rock 'n' roll rebels.

There's always an element of the lemming about any mass youth revolt. There are too many young men who are attracted by the idea that there's something good, noble and romantic about being spectacularly gunned down in the street by the forces of repression. It's the result of an over-exposure to *Viva Zapata, Butch Cassidy and the Sundance Kid* and all those crazy-mixed-up hoodlum movies where the good guy who's gone bad has to die in the last ten minutes to maintain morality and the punishment principle. This genre of movie has brainwashed too many into believing that running into a hail of bullets is an even better blaze of glory than going to one's death on a motorcycle or in a fast car. Morrison appealed to the souls of would-be martyrs by presenting himself as the biggest would-be martyr of all. If trouble and photographers approached at the same time, he would drop into a crucifixion pose. He was continuously and drunkenly offering himself for some kind of spectacular victimization.

Morrison's twin obsessions were the libertine cults of Dionysius and the kind of ancient fertility religions that ensured their followers survival and prosperity by choosing a monarch, (usually young, cute, male and virile), who would be sacrificed (usually by young, cute, nubile females) after seven years or some other suitably mystic period. Morrison's writing makes it clear that this was the role he wanted, if not for his total being, then certainly his stage persona: 'We are obsessed with heroes who live for us and whom we punish.' This wasn't merely a bleak observation, it was Morrison's job description and career goal. At the famous concert in Miami in 1969, which caused his arrest for lewd and lascivious behaviour, he played the victim to the hilt. He arrived on stage in beard and sunglasses, carrying a small white lamb like he was some dark, pre-Raphaelite messiah. He concluded by exposing himself to a howling crowd. His only logical next move would have been to abandon himself to the crowd and let them eat him alive. Instead, he abandoned himself to the police.

Even his leather clothes were made a part of the psychic cocktail. He was the Lizard King and he could do anything. That theoretically included the ability to shed his skin at the crucial moment and slip away before they could stretch him out on the altar and reach for the knife. (It's quite possible that the guilt for this cosmic deceit would have been enough on its own to force him to drink himself to death.) One of the clear perquisites of the Lizard King was that he was allowed free sexual rampage throughout the kingdom – a kind of blanket *droit de seigneur* – 'she was a princess/queen of the highway/he was a monster/black dressed in leather'.

Morrison had clearly given a good deal of thought to the psych/sex/freako trappings which go with a leather suit. Without doubt, he had evolved the kind of long, complex, floating theory that's the delight of the continuously loaded. Anyone who goes around calling himself the Lizard King is virtually compelled to take what might be called the reptile route. The reptile route is a loose cocktail of Jungian phallic symbolism and dinosaur fear – all that Carl Sagan stuff about how we all have this genetic memory from the time when dinosaurs not only ruled the earth but also liked to snack on our ancestors, the first cuddly little mammals.

This comes out of the cerebral blender as the explanation that, when you dress up in black leather, you've given yourself the approximation of a shiny reptile skin. When you confront other humans, they're filled with an echo of the fear felt by an early cuddly mammal faced with a hungry and carnivorous dinosaur. It's tortuous even for a pervert.

SMUT BY
NUMBERS

'**W**ipe that stupid expression off your face and strip naked.'

Obediently, he undressed. His hands were shaking slightly and he fumbled on the buttons of the dark grey business suit.

'Hurry up, you little worm, I don't have all day.'

She flexed the riding crop between black gloved fingers. When he'd removed the last of his clothing she nodded curtly.

'Now down on your knees, you worthless piece of slime.'

He did exactly as he was told, doubling over and pressing his forehead into the orange nylon shagpile of the hotel room carpet. She seemed to tower over him. The candlelight gleamed in the highlights of her black leather

outfit. It accentuated the smooth curves of her body, cold and hard and powerful. He wanted to reach out a hand and touch her. He could imagine the warm pink flesh under the cruel, austere leather; he ached for it but he didn't dare make a move. All he could do was stare at the pointed toe of her black patent, stiletto heeled boot. And then she was bending over him, fastening the straps, first to his wrists and then to his ankles.

'Raise your head.'

He prayed that she wasn't going to use the gag this time.

'Open your mouth, worm.'

There were no half-measures in this relationship.

You could call it generic pornography or smut

Leather night in Heaven. It's a London gay club, honest Reverend.

by numbers. The genders are infinitely interchangeable. Men on women, women on men, men on men, etc, etc. Homo, hetero, gay, lesbian, and possibly even the odd doberman. If you can conceive it, someone is probably publishing a magazine full of pictures of it. The great majority of commercial porno works on a fairly simple card index system. (Indeed, the operation of such a card index was Winston Smith's job in *1984*.) To create sleaze for either screen or print is pretty much an automatic process. One mixes and matches the genders and then runs down the standard menu of preferences, practices and deviations. You don't have to go too far before you run head-first into black leather – usually as one of the trappings of sado-masochism.

The problem with any discussion of sado-masochism is that you can immediately get into trouble. If you're a man, Christians and feminists go straight for your throat. If you're a woman, you'll also find Christians and feminists at your throat. The *Village Voice* has an on-going debate about whether lesbians who practice S&M merit a place in the feminist movement. In the same way there's a large section of the male Gay Liberation movement who appear to believe that the heavy leather cruisers with their shaved heads, mirrored shades and taste for fist-fucking are detrimental to the responsible gay image. On one side of the argument you'll hear the phrase 'a consentual sexual preference' while on the other there's angry talk of brutality, battering, rape and murder. In the centre, there's a lot of head scratching and a good deal of wonderment over how pleasure and pain actually can be an appealing sexual cocktail. The closest thing to an acceptable face of S&M is the professional dominatrix meting out clearly deserved punishment to the middle-aged, white, middle-class male for a couple of hundred of bucks an hour.

Despite the furore one thing remains clear – in fact, the furore really tends to confirm it – the images of sado-masochism exert a pervasive hothouse attraction to more of the population than many would care to admit. From *Vogue* to rock videos, it's almost impossible to get away from images of dominance and submission. S&M has so infiltrated pop culture that organizations like Woman Against Pornography suspect an actual conspiracy.

A perfect example of how sex may turn heads but S&M really snaps them round with a guilty start was the time in the early eighties when America held its breath over the Vicky Morgan sex tapes. Vicky Morgan was a top class hooker who had been the mistress of credit card czar and Ronald Reagan confidant Alfred Bloomingdale. When Bloomingdale died in 1982, Vicky felt assured of a much more than adequate life pension in gratitude for the services she'd rendered to the elderly multi-millionaire. Bloomingdale's wife, however, was having none of it. She went to court to make damn sure that Morgan was not going to set precedent in seven figure, posthumous palimony. With the judge leading the way, the ruling class closed ranks and Vicky was cut off without a penny. The world smiled and waited for her book to come out.

At that point, though, the rumour began to rapidly go around that Vicky had had the presence of mind to grab the video tapes. And not only sex tapes of Alfred's antics. Part of her duties was to play hostess at Washington whip and dog leash parties where prominent members of the Reagan administration got together to party and unwind with specially hired leather girls. Vicky also had this stuff on tape. Speculation bounded like Snoopy at suppertime. Who could be in the pictures? Meese? Clarke? Watt? Weinburger? Ann Burford? Surely not Ron himself? Grotesque humour was layered on the prurience. And then, a few months later, Vicky was dead. Supposedly murdered by her gay room-mate. A Los Angeles lawyer claimed that he had the tapes but quickly went to ground and finally decided that, no, maybe, he didn't have them after all, perhaps he'd only heard about them. Porn baron Larry Flynt also claimed ownership for a couple of days but, when the cops came knocking at the gates of his estate with a warrant, he too decided that he might have been a little confused. One way or another, the Reagan S&M tapes were gone. Maybe they'd never existed. Vicky Morgan's tapes joined the dead aliens in Hanger 18 as another mythological by-product of the global power conspiracy.

The reason for this lengthy digression is simply to underline the guilty fascination that

If you can imagine it, somebody is publishing pictures of it.

S&M holds for so many, and to lay the groundwork for at least a minimal explanation of why black leather clothes play such a major role as costumes in a sexual underground that, over the last two decades – indeed since Emma Peel and *The Avengers* – has been an increasing part of the risqué edge of mainstream fashion.

(If it's any consolation, it would seem that S&M exists in far more people's fantasies than their real-time sex, according to *Playboy's* fairly extensive 1983 sex survey. Only 5 per cent of their respondants had even engaged – or admitted to engaging – in any kind of pain-related sexual contact.)

If we try to pick our way through the mirror maze that leads to the real, psycho-sex significance of black leather and all that goes with it, the first thing we have to bear in mind is that one person's fetish may be another's anathema. Possibly the simplest way to pick a route is to go right back to basics.

We all know that black leather is sexy. You only have to walk down the street to realize this. Black leather, particularly form-fitting black leather, is a polished and reflective surface that tends to accentuate the natural contours of the body. It heightens the effect of any movement and therefore the impact of anything you might naturally have going for you. It brings out and extends the obvious. The same could be said about any reflective material from watered silk to vinyl but none are invested with quite the same deeply erotic significance. Clearly it isn't just the visual on its own that give black leather its impact. We have to look further to find the whole picture.

If it's not the visual, then all we have left is either the tactile, the symbolic or a combination of the two. The tactile appeal of black leather is possibly the strangest of all considerations. Leather is, of course, skin, a second dead skin that can be shed at will. In this, Jim Morrison was right on the money with his Lizard King fantasy. The average psychologist will tell you that the wearing of leather is a form of protection, possibly even a kind of desensitization. The living, vulnerable flesh is covered by an invulnerable dead hide. Emotionally, the leather wearer cannot be killed because, on the outside, he or she is already dead. In a similar way, on the other side of the relationship, the one who wants to touch and caress someone wearing leather is also looking for a degree of desensitization. The object of desire is covered in a dead skin. They are not quite mortal, not totally alive and therefore somehow less threatening than a full-blooded living partner who might make demands or require a greater degree of response or involvement than the leather lovers feel themselves capable.

Before, though, we wind ourselves all the way to necrophilia, it has to become obvious that once again we are talking about armour and the illusion of power that can be derived from that armour. We're back with twentieth century magic. The correlation between S&M and black leather is neither a matter of accentuation nor death. The connection is power. Just as black leather on the street can transform a teenage punk into Billy the Kid, black leather in the bedroom can change a systems analyst into the Princess of Darkness. The basis of any S&M relationship is a completely simplified analog of a power structure. The dominant partner has an absolute fantasy power over the submissive who, in turn, beyond the superficial pain and/or humiliation, experiences the almost womblike comfort of total attention and the total removal of any responsibility for the need to make sexual decisions.

There's a not inconsiderable section of the population that brands both the bravado of the punk on the street and the private dramas of S&M as the product of a pathetic and deep-seated inadequacy. The street punk, according to this mindset, isn't man enough to face the

One person's fetish may be another's anathema.

The more deviant the behaviour, the more the general public goes into shock.

world without his black leather jacket and his motorcycle boots. (And probably his angel dust, his switchblade, his pint of I.W. Harper as well.) In the same way, S&M practitioners aren't human enough to enjoy natural sex and have to resort to restraints and constrictions, straps, buckles, leather and high heels. The typically cited example is the withdrawn and twitching male masturbater with his bondage magazines, who gets it off to pictures of trussed women because he's too emotionally stunted to relate sexually to a real live person. At the other extreme, there was the advert placed in *Screw* magazine by a Detroit pro dominatrix during the 1980 Republican convention. Under a flattering picture of the lady, plying her trade in full costume, part of the copy read 'Don't let Carter whip your ass, let me do it!'

This is the favourite stereotype of all where S&M is concerned, the one that kept America on its toes during the potential Vicky Morgan scandal. There's a mass reassurance in the idea of the power brokers and the movers of millions on their knees in front of a costumed hooker, play-acting expiation of their sins with bondage and beatings. There's infinite comfort in the idea that our leaders are more distorted than we are, that their money and power hasn't made them happy, it's just made them painfully twisted. My problem here is that I've never really been able to subscribe to the inadequacy theory. It appears a little too close to just another attempt at drawing a line between clean sex and dirty sex. In the same way, I've never bought the idea that sexual preference is the sole result of some deep emotional imbalance, and I'm equally unable to believe the notion that the super rich are intrinsically unhappy.

Possibly one of the most damaging traits of Judeo-Christian culture, from stoning adultresses onwards, is to jump to the most punishingly negative sexual conclusions. Could it not be, when the president of a multinational corporation kneels in front of his favourite dominatrix in an anonymous room at the Hilton having paid for thongs and a thrashing, he's not expiating guilt, he's simply dabbling vicariously in the novelty of powerlessness on a strictly temporary basis. If he's not having the time of his life, he's certainly relaxing in a refreshingly different identity.

I'm sure there are individuals whose sexuality has been shaped by deprivations during their early upbringing ('My mother made me a homosexual' – 'If I gave her the wool, could she make me one?') but does that necessarily preclude those whose tastes have been shaped by their own imagination, curiosity and creative instinct?

Preaching, however, will do little to change the fact that the more deviant the behaviour, the more the general public goes into shock. Shock, is, of course, also a demonstration of vulnerability and it's been the major responsibility of any would-be counter culture from DaDa to hard core to go after that vulnerability at every chance they get. One of the time-honoured tactics is to take what was once bedroom-private and parade it on the street. In the fifties, it was blatant, teenage heterosex that hung them up; in the sixties it was dope, rock 'n' roll and fucking in the streets. The seventies advanced from androgyny to bondage.

In the world that has taken pop evolution from Frank Sinatra to Boy George and Doris Day to Marilyn Chambers, it's obvious that even Archie Bunker is quickly inured. This is why it was inevitable that the S&M trappings would eventually be dragged out of the closet and flourished in the face of the Saturday crowd at the shopping mall. When the black leather from Mistress Mara's Exclusive Dungeon cross-fertilized with the black leather sitting on the hoods of their Chevys drinking beer, you know the stylistic fun has started in earnest.

SWINGING SINGLES

The black leather jacket made the transition from the sixties to the seventies with little panache. But, then again, little did, with the possible exception of Richard Nixon and his wall-eyed cronies. For the counter culture, there was a sense of defeat, delay and a souring of ideals. *Easy Rider* may have been one of the last screen hits of the decade but everyone was well aware that its heroes, Wyatt and Billy, ended their search for America gunned down by rednecks on a Louisiana backroad. Darkness at the break of noon covered *even* the silver spoon. The drug underground that had once offered the certainty of a floral reworking of human nature lost its confidence and moved from psychedelics to amphetamines to barbiturates to heroin. It teetered on the edge of either burnout or addiction and, echoing the Grateful Dead, reflected on what a long strange trip it had been. The boys and girls in

the berets, buttons and boots had lost their revolution. The only survivors, the outlaw groups like the Weather Underground, the Angry Brigade, the Bader-Meinhoff embraced the grim rationale of terrorism. The FBI appeared to be systematically murdering or imprisoning the Black Panthers. Rock 'n' roll had lost its innocence. Jim Morrison was drinking himself to death in Paris and even the Hell's Angels were tainted by the killing and brutality at the Rolling Stones' Altamont free concert.

Of course, there were still plenty of black leather jackets around, but much of the magic seemed to have dissipated. Disappointed radicals still wore them as they sat in bars and wondered what went wrong. They were still the standard biker uniform, and a major costume for extrovert gay cruisers but somehow the flourish and swagger seemed to have flown.

A certain traditionalism was maintained by a lengthy bout of fifties' nostalgia, (a bout of nostalgia that, by 1984 had still not completely gone away). To some extent, it was triggered by Elvis Presley's 1968 NBC TV Special when, in an attempt to put a wasted decade of bikini fun pictures behind him, Elvis came out determinedly rocking in head to toe black leather. Fuelled by a basic yearning for simpler times, this late sixties/early seventies rock revival gave Britain Shakin' Stevens and America Sha Na Na. It also put Chuck Berry, Jerry Lee Lewis and the chronically sick Gene Vincent back on the bill at stadium rock shows. When all was added up, though, the lasting yield of the endeavour turned out to be little more than *American Graffiti,* a slew of James Dean T-shirts, the musical *Grease* and the TV show *Happy Days.* There was a great deal of money made, Henry Winkler became a

Life and art continue their romance. Peter Fonda in The Wild Angels *and real Hell's Angels under arrest in New Orleans.*

cult figure among the under-twelves, but it was hardly what amounted to a mass movement.

What was much worse was, while the fifties were being candy-coloured on stage and screen, the leather jacket was being co-opted in the high street and the shopping mall. The leather jacket myth had been so heavily promoted in the media that word had finally filtered through to the tranquillized suburbs where, to all but the kids – who'd probably run away years earlier anyway – the youth revolt meant Sonny and Cher. A denatured version of the leather jacket was saying young and now to people who were old and then, if not actually, at least spiritually. Boutiques and even chain stores sported racks of decidedly unmagical leathers where once there'd only been windbreakers, sport coats and maybe the odd Nehru jacket. They were dinky approximations with funny lapels, apologetic zippers and a tendency to fall apart in a matter of weeks. They came in black – but they also came in blue, tan, bottle green and burgundy. Their wearers combined them with double knit bell bottoms, patterned body shirts, Gucci loafers, gold chains, chest hair, oversized watches and little red European sports cars.

This new mutation rapidly became standard issue for the swinging single on the make, the kind of individual who believed that seduction was a matter of Sammy Davis, talk of astrology and a couple of bottles of Mateus Rosé. Later, though, the ersatz leather jacket would start to appear on the golf course and would eventually filter down to be the garb of inadequate petty criminals, John Travolta's day wear in *Saturday Night Fever* and the dress for success for individuals who wear mirror shades and sell quaaludes in the men's room at discos. The genus still survives today in the costumes of soap operas and those who dress accordingly.

Fortunately for all of us, you can't keep a good counter-culture down. It's true that the

glitter glam extravaganza of the early seventies initially did nothing at all for the black leather jacket and, indeed, for a while, it would be totally eclipsed by gold codpieces and twelve-inch clear plexiglass platform boots with live goldfish swimming around inside the soles. But glam is still relevant in this context, in that it set up the situation that would lead to black leather's most massive come-back.

The generation that came of teenage in the immediate wake of the hippies was confronted with a set of unique problems. In terms of adolescent rebellion, the sixties had just about covered the spectrum. The stoned be-ins of the inner ring flower children, the narcotic excess and amateur satanism of the Rolling Stones all the way to the bombing campaigns of the Weather Underground had left few avenues through which to demonstrate a healthy contempt for maturity and authority. Just to complicate matters there was still considerable debris left behind from the previous decade, ranging from panhandling long-haired derelicts to a rock 'n' roll elite who considered that, since they'd survived the sixties, they should now continue for the rest of their lives in an unchallengeable pop pantheon.

Tired of the grabs and starting to contemplate what unpleasantness might be revealed in the real world during the second half of the seventies, youth culture realized that it would have seriously to rethink its attitudes to image and street style. In the long run, glitter could be nothing more than a fad and while it might certainly teach a number of useful lessons, a more aggressive, hard-edged look was better suited to what appeared to be deteriorating times. The punks were the product of this realization and with them the black leather jacket came solidly back into its own.

In jacket art the sublime turns to the ridiculous; in rock'n'roll the ridiculous turn to Kiss.

THE NEW
BARBARIANS

I n Wardour Street, which runs north-south through London's Soho, there's a pub called the Ship. Its clientele is split pretty much between the film industry, musicians and their entourages and the odd wandering tourist. This is hardly surprising in view of the fact that it's on the same block as a number of the major film distributors and also the Marquee Club. The Marquee has been a major springboard for British rock 'n' roll since the early sixties. The Rolling Stones played there; when the Who made their mark

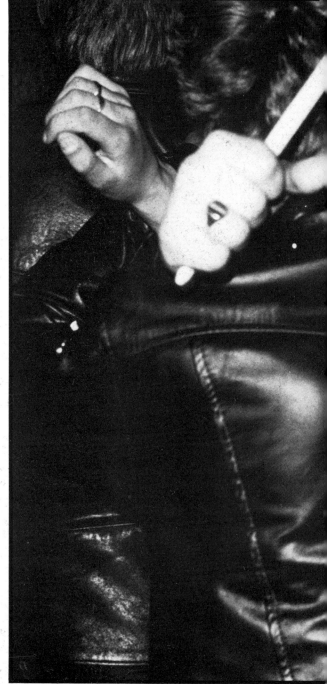

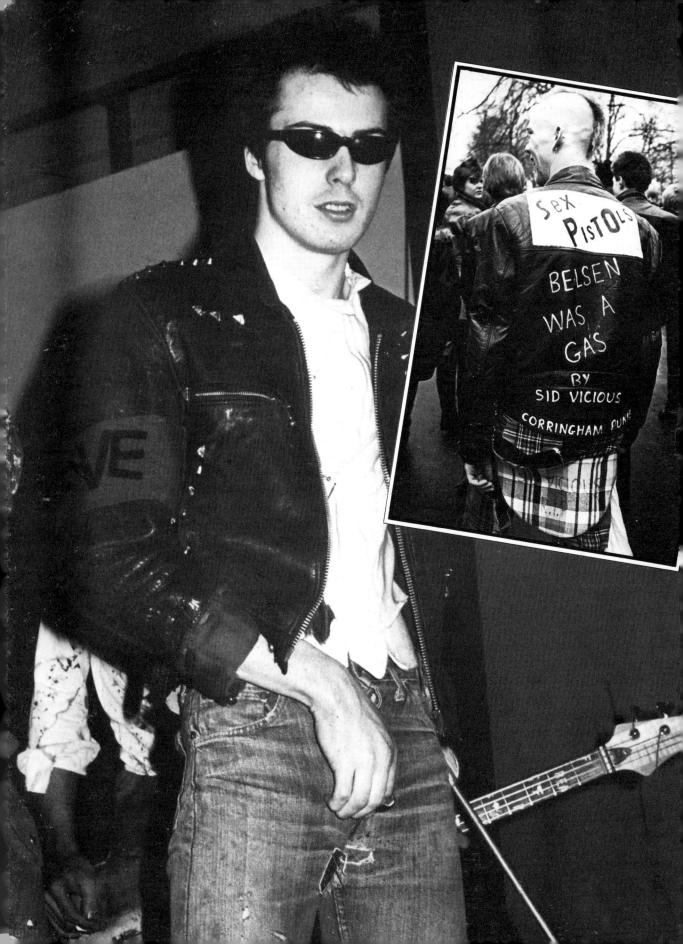

SeX PisTOLS

BELSEN
WAS A
GAS
BY
SID VICIOUS

CORRINGHAM PUNX

with a Tuesday night residency, the club became a matter of legend. Right through to today it continues to be a showcase for the young and the hopeful. The landlord of the Ship and his staff have witnessed and eventually tolerated every fad that has emerged from rock 'n' roll and its attendant youth culture. They've weathered the Mods and Rockers' conflicts, they'd seen the flower children come and go and they'd even played host to David Bowie. What usually worried them more than even the weirdest of rock fans were the tartan hordes who'd descend on London for the biennial England-Scotland soccer match and usually try and raze the town after the game. On those nights, they closed the bar. But when I walked in for a drink on a damp night in late 1976 they seemed to be thinking about closing and there wasn't a tartan scarf for miles.

I forget which band had been playing the Marquee. It was one of the early punk emergences – something like X-Ray Spex, Sham 69, Subway Sect – and the Ship had had its first experience of true punk excess. According to those still sitting around talking about it, among the crowd who'd come in to drink and hang out before the show had been a leather-clad punkette leading her friend on a dog collar and leash. Her friend – also female – had been dressed in shoes, stockings, suspenders, a clear plastic garbage sack and a belt. The landlord had become apoplectic as he'd thrown them out. He'd yelled, he'd turned red and he'd sweated. He'd seen Jimi Hendrix blasted out of his mind, he'd experienced Keith Moon in full cry but he'd never seen anything like this. The affrontery was absolute and he was absolutely affronted.

One idea that the punks carried forward from the glitter kids was that everyone could

Even years after, on the toilet walls of western democracy, Sid still lives!

do it. With the hardening of attitude that seemed to come around the middle of the decade, though, it was no longer a matter of aspiring to an illusion of fame. The punk pose was that illusions were bullshit. They weren't starfuckers, they were iconoclasts. No more stars. No more idols or leaders or mass market heroes. Any band in a garage with three chords and two Japanese guitars was as good as Led Zeppelin. Some even demanded an end to rock 'n' roll. They were the goon squad and they were coming to town. Beep beep. No future. No quarter. Anarchy.

Even though they would in time develop their fair share of appendages and accessories, there was a stripped down feel to the punks that had much more to do with the fifties than the sixties. They'd cut their hair and greased it into stiff, angry spikes. Some shaved their heads. The basic outfit was as basic as you can get: black leather jacket, black jeans and heavy boots. They brought pop music back from the forty minute voyages of exploration of Cream or the Grateful Dead and returned it to its original two and half minute, three chord mode.

Punk, on the ground floor, was a detailed investigation of terminal ugliness that boldly went where no culture had gone before. Particularly in London they even stepped outside any conventional idea of civilization during the early punk heyday by starting a vogue for cosmetic mutilation. The safety pin that was to provide so much ammunition for middle-aged comedians was thrust through lips, nostrils and ears. Chains were hung from nose ring to ear-ring. Hands, arms, torsos, sexual organs and even faces were adorned with crude jailhouse-style tattoos, while make-up more frequently disfigured than enhanced and no garment was worth a damn until it was ripped and torn.

Although nobody seemed to notice at the time, the punks had a highly developed sense

of pop symbolism. It was only natural for a generation that had lived, cradle to puberty, with total television and were gathering images before they could walk. The mean punk birth date, somewhere around 1960, exactly coincided with the time when the television set was being universally accepted as an electronic baby sitter. This not only left them with a huge subconscious reservoir of pop symbols but also a total lack of reserve about incorporating any available one into their image. New York singer Richard Hell claims to have invented the ripped T-shirt that, for a while, was a corner stone of punk fashion. It is, in fact, more likely that Hell, either consciously or unconsciously, saw the torn undershirt on Marlon Brando as Stanley Kowalski in *A Streetcar Named Desire,* liked what he saw, made it part of his professional wardrobe and started to promote it as a look along with the promotion of himself and his music.

The punks use of symbolism provided a very comprehensive guide to their basic philosophy. This was fortunate since they generally nurtured an almost overwhelming lack of articulacy. Where the hippies would babble on for hours about their spiritual and political aspirations, the punks tended to scowl, grunt abuse and, when their deliberately restricted attention span ran out, become physically aggressive. The basic black jeans, torn T-shirt and boots was, as I have already suggested, a very direct backward glance to a romantic memory of the zip gun gangs of the fifties. In this, they defined themselves as traditional scum. Traditional, however, was far from good enough. At the start there was a rash of Nazi regalia; it went hand in hand with the self-mutilation. Most quickly discovered that that particular piece of visual assault had become timeworn since the bike clubs had adopted it a dozen or more years earlier. The

In both punk and post-punk, the black leather jacket became a part of street fashion.

majority quickly gave up the entire idea while the ones who kept their swastikas and SS deathheads felt compelled to go all the way into some variety of neo-fascist nastiness. Punk was one of the few youth movements that could stand a political polarization within its ranks (updated Nazis at one extreme and card carrying Trotskyists at the other) without tearing itself apart.

Not that punk ever promoted itself as a cohesive movement. It accepted that Western civilization was but a red button away from fragmentation and collapse and that it was a mirror to this desperate future. The only way to react to this belief that the apocalypse was just over the hill was to cultivate a full set of negatives – anger, violence and a locked-in hostility. This was an extreme reaction to the youth attitudes of the sixties. Peace 'n' love had been tried and proved itself a sick joke. The punks held the hippies – their elder brothers and sisters, or even their parents – in total contempt for what they saw as their failure. The Sex Pistols summed it up in two words: 'No future.'

More than any generation since World War II, they saw themselves as in need of personal armour against the end of everything. Black leather and studs weren't nearly enough. The basics had to be decorated with even more potent symbols. Many looked to the straps, buckles, spikes and collars of S&M equipment. Strips of rag would be arbitrarily tied around thigh and forearm. Garbage became jewellery. Some adopted the Anarchist A inside a circle. Others took up with the red star and hammer and sickle. The Clash favoured mismatched battledress inspired by the TV news terrorists. Even punk dancing became totally anti-sensual. The Pogo that eventually mutated into the Slam was and is such a ritual of stylized but still mindless violence that it was hard to tell a hardcore dance party from a Saturday night barroom brawl. The punks needed so much protection that they became atavistic, almost feral. Instead of merely wanting to be a new set of tough teenagers, they saw themselves as the new barbarians.

If you want to change your total identity, a very good first move is to change your name. This was possibly one of the major punk innovations that clearly indicated their desire to get out from under a crashing civilization. Not content with dressing for apocalypse, they also demanded to be known as Jane Suck, Lydia Lunch, Johnny Rotten or Sid Vicious. With the exception of a couple of dozen rock stars, nothing like it had ever been seen before. In thirty years, the rebellion without a cause had reached the point of seemingly total alienation.

If the punks' primary motivation was to shock, they went about it in exactly the right way. The general furore that accompanied their first unveiling surpassed that that greeted Elvis Presley, the Rolling Stones or the first flourish of the hippies. An English father of four was reputed to have smashed his TV when the Sex Pistols appeared for the first time on a British talk show. The Los Angeles Police Department was accused of conducting a well-defined vendetta against the surf punks of Venice and Huntingdon Beach. Neo-fascist thugs attempted to kill or at least maim Johnny Rotten outside a London pub. Even those who should have known better were mildly horrified. Sixties radicals grunted and scowled. 'The only punks I ever heard about were the ones who let themselves get butt-fucked in jail.' The rock establishment protested vocally that punks 'were getting 99 per cent of the press and selling 1 per cent of the records'.

Like most cultural sensations, punk was dismissed as a nine day wonder. By far the bulk of rock critics were visibly relieved when the New Wave restored traditional verities like craft, creativity and pretty faces. Somehow they felt more comfortable with Elvis Costello and the Attractions than Darby Crash and the Germs. Punk, however, didn't die despite the constant death notices. Interestingly, it also didn't remain static, proving that it was not, as so many imagined, the end of some sociological branch line. Punk continued. On one level it mutated to the greater excesses of hardcore, on another it softened and diffused and became a part of the general look of street fashion. In both cases, the black leather jacket went right along with it.

If you draw a line from Gene Vincent through Jim Morrison and then project it into the seventies, you arrive at Sid Vicious. If James Dean was the identikit fifties teenager, Sid Vicous was the identikit seventies punk. In his ripped black jeans, black leather jacket, torn T-shirt or no shirt at all, he'd taken this particular school of rock star image to a minimalist extreme. My own first-hand memories of Vicious are less than fond. I recall a ragged, bleary, slack-faced, near comatose young thug whom I avoided like the plague and who, after a bunch of Carlsberg Special Brews, developed a penchant for hitting the people nearest him with the padlock and chain he always wore around his neck. These attacks frequently came without either warning or provocation. My observations hardly matter here, however. Since his death by heroin OD in a lower Manhattan apartment following his arrest for the alleged murder of his demented girlfriend Nancy Spungen, he became something that was far greater than the sum total of either his achievements, his image, his personality or even his death.

It wasn't until the summer of 1980 that I really became aware of the cult that had formed around Sid. I was standing around in this record store thumbing through the 'S groups' stack and thinking about nothing in particular. At first I didn't notice the two young girls standing with their backs to me. Not noticing them was partially deliberate. They were in that transitional stage between sub-teen and puberty that makes it necessary for them to fluctuate between smothered giggles and worldly-wise street drawl. It made me nervous when I was twelve and still does to this day.

They were blowing Bubblicious and carefully regarding the cover of an album: *Sid Sings*. This was when I began to take notice. They were treating the thing with the kind of reverence that betrayed them as true fans. It was an icon. Plainly they regarded Sid Vicious with the damp fervour I thought was normally directed toward Leif Garret or Scott Baio.

I knew I was in the presence of something I had never come across before. These were Sid's people. They were no left-over junior punkettes from two summers earlier. They had no real relationship to new wave music. They'd never find their way to the Mudd Club. They were simply devoted to Sid. I decided to go to a bar and think about all this. In the men's room there was a graffito: 'Sid Lives.' I started to remember all the other bathrooms and urban walls on which I'd seen Sid Vicious graffiti: I realized there was one hell of a lot of it. Sid's people had to be a force to be numerically reckoned with.

It took me some time to realize what I was confronting here. Sid had no more to do with music than James Dean had to do with the movies. The late Sid Vicious is now in the business of altars, imagery and hallowed magazine clippings. There has been nothing like this for a long time. Even the hyperbole over the end of Elvis was only the final act of something that had been rolling on for twenty years. The Sid Vicious cult was all new.

In order to understand the Sid cult we have to go back to James Dean. There's no parallel with the Rolling Stones or the Beatles; they were accessible and too human. Janis and Jimi won't do. Jim Morrison almost made it; he tried hard enough to be a cult figure but death in exile and obesity disqualified him. Maybe the closest thing to a true sixties icon was Charles Manson, but that's a stone best left unturned.

No. James Dean has to be the ideal example. He made three films and an auto wreck. For the fifties it was the perfect teenage dream: he got to be a movie star and then died in a fast car. That qualified for Valhalla. If you wanted to get anthropological about it, you could cite Dean as one of those pagan symbols. Jim Morrison was always aspiring to: a fertility sacrifice – the youthful god-king who must die so the rest may survive. Mind you, the idea turns a little nasty when we return to Sid Vicious. Dean was a movie star in an auto wreck. Vicious was a rock star in a murder/suicide scandal.

Sid's career was brief. He hung around with John Lydon, invented his name, replaced Glen Matlock in the Sex Pistols (because Matlock could play and he couldn't), played a disastrous US tour, maybe murdered Nancy and OD'd. Is this how the teenage dream has evolved in 25 years? Two and a half decades of twentieth century living have turned the stuff of True Romance into something out of Genet.

It was often said that James Dean was an anthology of adolescent rebellion in his time, and in creating that image he laid the groundwork for much of the youth upheavals of the sixties. Perhaps Vicious is simply another updated and escalated anthology. Dean was from the era of the Sabre jet, Sid Vicious inhabited the world of the cruise missile. What upheavals will be laid at Sid's door are still a matter of speculation.

On a slightly deeper level, Dean had a childlike quality, an infant morality that raged at the compromises of his parents' world. Sid, on the other hand, had a puritan innocence that was totally outside morality. Violence and downers provided him with an easy amoral detachment that came as close as possible to removing him from a corrupt and unendurable world.

SAVAGE
SKINS

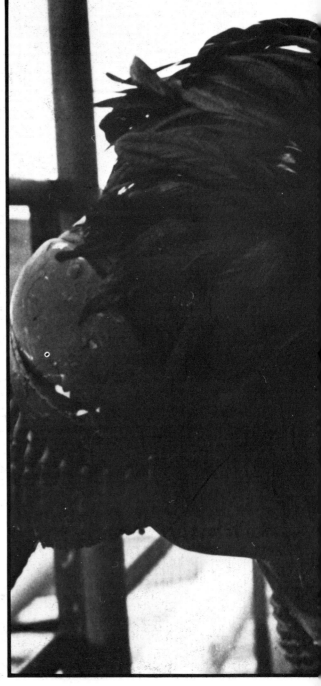

When Robert DeNiro, playing the disturbed Travis Bickle in the movie *Taxi Driver*, shaves his head into a Mohican haircut, it's a clear signal from director Martin Scorsese that Bickel's personality is well down the road to decay and that it's only a matter of time before he turns homicidal. With perverse relish, the post-punk hardcore kids adopted it as the next great haircut. In a single move, they not only suggested to passers-by that they, too, were in some collective personality breakdown, and that it might only be a matter of time before they too became homicidal, but they

also brought a noticeable tribalism to what was already a fairly barbaric image. There has to be some discussion as to whether a guy with a huge cockatoo crest of pink hair rising from an otherwise shaved scalp is strictly a part of civilization as we know it. The new barbarians were forming up into definable tribes, and the black leather jacket was moving into the realm of post-apocalypse science fiction.

There's a minor convention in post-apocalypse science fiction that suggests how, during World War III, the northern hemisphere will go down in nuclear flames but Australia will either survive or, at least, linger for an extra year or so, waiting for to be irradiated. One of the earliest manifestations of this idea was Nevil Shute's novel *On the Beach*, later filmed by Stanley Kramer with Gregory Peck, Ava Gardner, Fred Astaire and Anthony Perkins. In this, middle class Aussies await deferred atomic doom with varying degrees of controlled hysteria. That was the 1959 version. In 1980, we had *Mad Max*, and that was something very different.

Mad Max was director George Miller's first view of Australia after a global holocaust. In this, black leather clad speed cops in GT sports cars chase fairly conventional gangs of bikers and hot-rodders. It had a few laughs; a few characters die hideously; the cop hero (Max, played by Mel Gibson) finds his wife and child have been raped and murdered by motorcycle desperadoes and, in the finale, Max leaves one of the perpetrators with a choice of sawing off his own arm or being burnt to death in a gasoline fire. Taken on face value, *Mad Max* would have been little more than an interesting minor hybrid of science fiction and the car chase genre. In the scheme of things it was up there with *Hell's Angels on Wheels* or *The Hills Have Eyes* but it was

Mel Gibson as Mad Max, the 1980s fantasy of apocalypse film.

certainly no *Deathrace 2000*, and would certainly have remained merely a listing in *Movies on TV* if George Miller had not been given a second shot at the concept.

Mad Max II – released in the USA as *The Road Warrior* – is as crucial to the development of style in the 1980s as *The Wild One* is to the development of style in the fifties. It's possibly more important. Where *The Wild One* was basically a compendium of early biker styles and hipster attitudes, Miller, in his 1981 second shot, took the prevailing attitudes of punk/hardcore and projected them into a simple but comprehensive fantasy. In a barren, post-nuclear desert, savage but motorized tribes fight over the last of the gasoline. Max (again played by Mel Gibson) is now a bitter, antisocial loner in a leather suit and a Gene Vincent-style steel leg brace. His leathers are so overlaid with reinforcements and padding that they become an overt version of late twentieth century plate armour. He's Clint-like in his taciturn, slit eyed misanthropy. Apparently he has taken both the murder of his family and the fall of civilization extremely personally. A small dingo is his only friend and even that is killed half way through the picture.

A bunch of unreconstructed hippies – you can tell they're hippies because they wear oatmeal-coloured clothes, headbands and noble expressions – have a considerable quantity of gasoline. They'd like to move the gas and set up a colony on the coast. Unfortunately they are surrounded by the worst bunch of bad guys – the hordes of the Lord Humungus – that ever straddled a bike or drove a custom car or a dune buggy. For our purposes, the rest of the plot hardly matters (in fact, the hippies ask Max to help them move their gas; he refuses at first but in the end saves the day and then vanishes into the dust, proving that even bitterness can't bury a True Hero); what really counts is the style of these bad guys. In the Lord Humungus and his people, we see the basic black leather motorcycle gang transformed into the ultimate savage, nomadic tribe. In his attempt to portray these characters as the outer limits of barbarous scum, Miller plundered the whole of pop culture and beyond for accessories and visual symbols. The American Indians provided breech cloths, leggings and Mohawk-style scalp-locks. The wide world of sport was good for ice hockey masks and NFL shoulder armour. Heavy metal and S&M contributed elaborate confections of belts, buckles, straps and studs. When Charlie Manson dreamed of taking over the world during the final days of Armageddon with his dune buggy attack batallions there was no way that even his most fevered and vengeful acid vision could have exceeded George Miller's creation by anything but weight of numbers.

As well as being angrily, comic book awesome, *Mad Max II* also had a nastily romantic plausibility. Take away civilization and what have you got? Cannibal Apaches on motorcycles? Well maybe. It was as good a guess as any. Where *The Wild One* provided a compendium of delinquent styles, *Mad Max II* was a compendium of delinquent fantasies. A post-punk variation of *Tomorrow Belongs to Me*. What if the rest of the world went away and I was free to ride around the desert on my Vincent Black Shadow and kill people with the steel crossbow built into my leather wristband. Oh boy. Beats the hell out of annoying folks in bars.

Back in the real world there was no mistaking the movie's appeal. It pointed to one possible direction for the next phase in teenrabble fashion. At the same time as Boy George experimented with a perversely rummage sale androgyny that was a mid-point meeting between Ziggy Stardust and Charlie's Aunt, the leather jacket consciousness went increasingly feral. The hardcore kids who, during the first couple of years of the eighties had seemed to be taking on a bullet-headed

drabness, began to return to more flamboyant accessories. Mohican haircuts became towering creations in fluorescent colours. Rock singer Billy Idol rebuilt a career that had faltered after the break-up of his first band, Generation X, on an image almost completely borrowed from Mel Gibson in *Mad Max II* and a voice borrowed from Jim Morrison. Indeed, in melodramatically narcissistic rock videos, he made it clear that he was the sneering, albino version of the same delinquent Armageddon. (Just to help matters, the first video in this series, *Dancing With Myself* was produced by Tobe Hooper, the man responsible for the gory classic *The Texas Chainsaw Massacre*.)

In his second video, *Rebel Yell*, Billy Idol wears a red and black leather jacket that had quite literally been shredded. All that appeared to remain were a couple of shoulder seams, a collar and a lot of flying fringes. To the old-time biker purist, the idea of putting a knife to a leather jacket was an unthinkable act. In reality it was just the latest form of customizing, of bringing the standard model jacket more in line with the character of both the individual and the times.

Although, on the surface, there was something a little kamikaze about the extensive slicing up of the basic garment, leather jackets had, in fact, been being scissored since the sixties bike clubs and urban street gangs had developed a fetish for cutting the sleeves off anything they could get their hands on. Even that, though, manifested a degree of recklessness. The kid who cut the sleeves off his leather to display his biceps and tattoos was announcing to the world that he was letting go of a part of his armour, ie he was such a bad motherfucker that he'd give the enemy a free shot, one hand behind his back, so to speak. For a while in the mid-sixties the Hell's Angels made something of a big deal out of how they would totally eschew the wearing of leather. They were so goddam tough that they'd drive through the weather and even take spills onto

'Hey, look, I'm taking off my armour'.

the road surface with only denim to protect them. It was a flourish, but the realities of motorcycling swiftly reasserted themselves and the Angels brought their jackets back out of the closet.

Billy Idol's shredded jacket was simply more of the same bravado. Hey, look at me, I'm crazy, I'm taking off all my armour. This was also the message of *Mad Max II*. In this post-holocaust desert there's no such thing as courage; there are only differing levels of crazy, self-destructive rage. You worked yourself into a beserker frenzy and then hurled yourself in front of a truck. (The one character called on to take a disinterested risk is Max himself and, in this, he remains a traditional if minimal hero.) The youthful enthusiasm for George Miller's fantasies sent one very clear signal to the rest of the world. Once upon a time the message of the kid in black leather jacket was that he perceived a hostile gulf between himself and his peer group and the grown-up world. Today it's been taken a stage further. The kid now believes that you need to be crazy to grow up in a world like this.

The key to understanding the eighties and the culture yet to come has to be the word 'fragmentation'. Ever since the break-up of the mass consumer standardization that came with the post World War II boom, increasingly smaller subdivisions have demanded that they should be recognized as separate life-styles with their own looks, their own specialist tastes, their own humour and even, at times, their own philosophy and morality. The progress of magazine publishing from 1950 to (say) 1980 provides a perfect model for our

Below and right: *street style and style from designer Katherine Hamnett.*

Ever since haute couture *lost its monopoly grip on popular fashion, somewhere around 1962, the garment industry has consistently pillaged the style of the street.* Left: *a leather 'blouson' by Sonia Rykiel.* Top right: *a Montana design and* bottom right: *a jacket by Gianni Versace.*

BLACK TIE

VIP

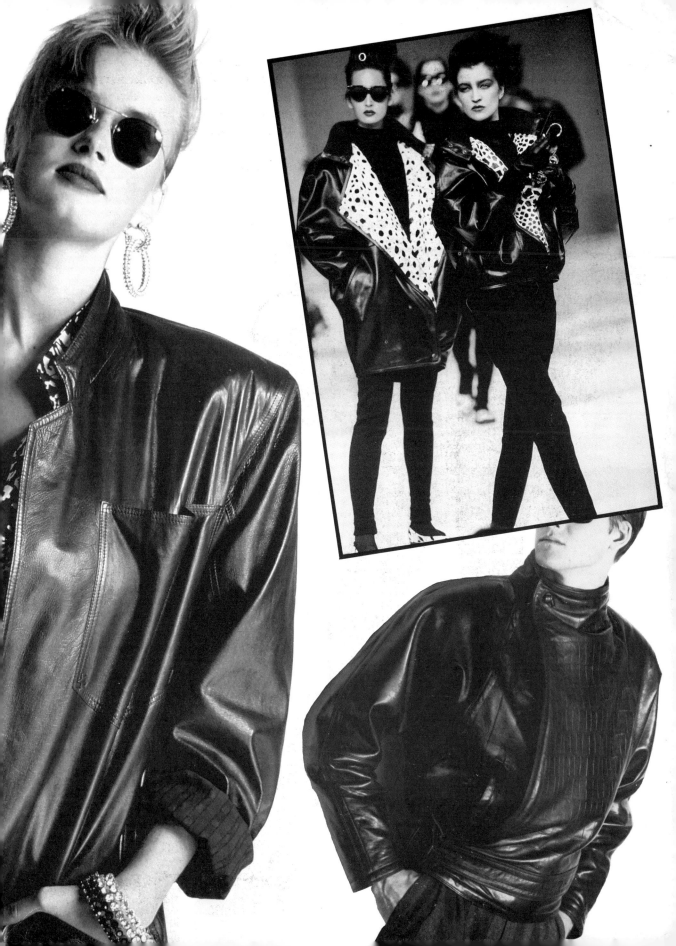

The style of the street, however, is a few stages removed from the style of the sexual underground. It took iconoclasts like Vivienne Westwood and Betsy Johnson to borrow images from the fetishist and the dominatrix. Once the ground was broken, though, there was no stopping them. Top centre: *designs by Jean Paul Gaultier and* bottom centre: *a design by Gianni Versace.*

mutating and subdividing culture. In the early fifties there were a handful of huge family entertainment magazines – *Life, Look, The Saturday Evening Post.* Then the big magazines faltered and over the next thirty years the corner news-stand was taken over by thousands of specialist publications, until today it's pretty much safe to say that if you can imagine it, somebody is probably publishing a magazine about it. Television has gone through a similar transformation. In 1950, the average American town had two, maybe three television stations. Today, with cable, it can have something between thirty and forty. Add on a satellite earth station and the number of available channels runs into hundreds.

What has happened to major communications systems is only a very simplified reflection of what has gone down in the culture as a whole. Even though many of us try to ignore the almost overwhelming diversity and pretend that there's still some degree of cultural homogeneity, we live in a world where a simple thing like rock 'n' roll music can encompass Nick Cave and Jerry Lee Lewis, where religion can mean anything from a slickly rabid fundamentalist TV preacher to a lobotomized Moonie selling roses on the airport. Only electoral politics flies in the face of all this plurality, having rendered itself down to a media spectacle of sub-conscious response.

As always, the black leather jacket provides a perfect illustration. Over these few humble pages we've watched it thread its way through the history of the last seventy years. We saw how it started out as a totally utilitarian garment designed for work and combat and how it was quickly invested with psychological, social, sexual and even magical significance. We saw how, during the youth explosion of the fifties, it became the virtual uniform of the bad kids. From that point on it spread outward through an increasing

number of subgroups of the main counter-culture until it reached the point where, at the time of writing, it seems that virtually everyone can incorporate some variation into their wardrobe. The heavy metal kids claim it for their own and wear it with long hair, a Judas Priest tour shirt and Nike running shoes. Rockabilly kids also claim it as their own and wear it in exaggerated imitation of the fifties. In the movie *Purple Rain,* Prince has his own somewhat Byronic version for the motorcycle sequences. His major rival, Michael Jackson, started out echoing James Dean in a red leather jacket, switched back to black for a Pepsi commercial but now seems to decorate everything he owns with tinsel epaulettes, gold braid and fake decorations fit only for a Ruritarian romp, that tend to make him look like a young, skinny, Third World dictator.

Standard bikers wear the standard bike drag and the jackets get more worn, wrinkled and interesting right along with the faces of their owners. Yuppies occasionally court disaster by assuming a leather jacket in the hope that it will lend them a raffish air while climbing out of the Volvo on the mall parking lot. On the gay strips the black leather jacket continues to hold its own, possibly more than ever now Ronald Reagan has reclaimed the Marlboro Man look. Duran Duran maintain a variation of the normal rock 'n' roll theme with a suitably French-style blouson. Investment counsellors who were once sixties radicals still keep their old black leather jackets in the closet in the same way that veterans hang onto their service uniforms. He's sure he's never going to need it again but in a world where nothing is ever certain you never can tell. Young boys who've either taken their savings or conned their parents and are standing in the local Army and Navy store buying their first leather jacket still feel as though they're going through a rite of passage.

The black leather jacket continues. At times it looks like it will go on forever.